CREVE COEUR
T 26399

P9-DOG-350

FIREFIGHTER CAREER STARTER

CREVE COEUR PUBLIC LIBRARY DIST.

A35520 324450

DATE DUE

JUN 24 13	

by Mary Masi

LearningExpress ◆ New York

Copyright © 1998 Learning Express, LLC.

All rights reserved under International and Pan-American Copyright Conventions. Published in the United States by LearningExpress, LLC, New York.

Library of Congress Cataloging-in-Publication Data

Firefighter career starter: finding and getting a great job.
      p.   cm.—(Career starters)
    ISBN 1–57685–112–5
        1. Fire extinction—Vocational guidance—United States.
I. LearningExpress (Organization) II. Series.
TH9119.F566   1998
363.37'023—dc21   98–6408
                                        CIP

Printed in the United States of America
9 8 7 6 5 4 3 2 1
First Edition

Regarding the Information in this Book
Every effort has been made to ensure accuracy of directory information up until press time. However, phone numbers and/or addresses are subject to change. Please contact the respective organization for the most recent information.

For Further Information
For information on LearningExpress, other LearningExpress products, or bulk sales, please call or write to us at:
      LearningExpress™
      900 Broadway
      Suite 604
      New York, NY 10003
      212-995-2566

LearningExpress is an affiliated company of Random House, Inc.

ISBN 1-57685-112-5

7 85555 85112 2

FOREWORD

WHY BECOME A FIREFIGHTER?

by William Gates,
New York City Fire Captain, Retired

You only come this way once in life. Firefighters know this, and they make the most of it.

Choosing to become a firefighter can only be described as embarking on a great adventure. But why become a firefighter in the first place? Who in their right mind would want to be exposed to these kinds of extreme conditions:

- Performing an aerial ladder, tower ladder, or rope rescue, several stories above the ground. The ladder swaying, making it difficult to perform. Knowing the rope will hold you, hoping it will hold two people.
- Inhaling dangerous smoke, sometimes containing polyvinyl chloride, asbestos, carbon monoxide, or other chemicals that are harmful and whose effects are cumulative.
- Crawling down a long, dark, smoky hallway with a charged hand line, facing intense heat at shoulder height. Not being able to see

because of the heat and smoke. Advancing the hose line with 60 pounds of pressure per square inch at the nozzle, trying to make it to that apartment or rear bedroom where someone may be trapped, knowing that seconds and minutes count.

♦ Racing up six or seven flights of stairs to the fire floor, wearing bunker gear and carrying 50 or 60 pounds of equipment, facing exhaustion, heat stroke—even death.

I have given you reasons not to become a firefighter. Now let me tell you why you should!

First of all, it's one of the best jobs in the world. I have over 33 years of experience as a firefighter. I've responded to almost 27,000 alarms—all of them on the line with the men and women of one of the greatest fire departments in the world. There is no doubt they are the most intelligent, kind, honest, caring, generous, talented, and physically fit people ever.

When I was a young man, I was working for the Federal Reserve Bank of New York, decoding foreign cablegrams. It was a job I hated. My father thought a civil service job would offer decent wages, good working conditions, health benefits, and the chance to retire while still fairly young. I passed both the police and firefighter tests, and was called at almost the same time as a candidate for both jobs. I chose, after careful consideration, to listen to my father's advice and accept the position of probationary firefighter. I have never looked back.

While waiting for my appointment, I was told to report to a local firehouse in my neighborhood: Engine Company 239 in South Brooklyn. The then-Fire Commissioner thought it was a good idea for us first to become an auxiliary firefighter so we could learn something about fire prevention before being appointed. Along with about 10 other candidates, I reported for a lecture about fire prevention, signing in on the company journal at the firehouse watch desk.

About 15 minutes into the lecture, loud bells began to sound, the lights became much brighter, the huge firehouse doors opened to the outside world, and men began sliding down shining brass poles. Like the snap of a finger, the pumper engine roared to life, moving quickly forward to the street, as the firefighters, dressed in their firefighting gear, jumped on board. The huge red machine accelerated quickly, its siren and bell echoing off the brownstones and tenements of South Brooklyn on the way to its coded destination. The enormous doors on the apparatus floor closed with a boom, but I could still hear all the sounds slowly disappearing toward downtown Brooklyn. All of 30 seconds had passed; I was stunned, impressed—and I knew that's what I wanted to be a part of.

The benefits of being a New York City Firefighter are a 20-year retirement at half-pay, unlimited sick leave, and 26 vacation days when you become a first-grade firefighter after five years. The starting salary is approximately $29,000, reaching about $50,000 after five years. Dental and medical benefits are included. In a word, fairly generous for the hardest working of New York City professionals. But if we consider their contribution towards society, they should be paid more!

But you don't become a firefighter just for the money; it's more than that—much, much more. There is a bond that is shared as in no other profession—split-second decisions, forceful entry into apartments and homes searching for life, rescuing the injured or unconscious, overhauling the fire area to make sure the fire is out and any extension of the fire is found and extinguished.

Conditions at a fire can be brutal, with multiple injuries, people screaming for missing or trapped loved ones. Firefighters returning to their quarters after a fire are often exhausted, but they must prepare for the next alarm. If they haven't suffered any injuries, they must change into dry uniforms, replace defective equipment and depleted air masks, and clean their tools. Once their reports are updated, they must notify the dispatcher that they are in service. After an unusual fire or incident, a fresh pot of coffee is made, and the officer of a truck or engine company will have the firefighters critique it: Who did what? Could we have done it safer? Faster? Better?

When you leave the firehouse after a day or night tour, you feel good about yourself. You might have helped save someone on that tour, or put out a fire. Over the years, I have seen firefighters approach greatness with their courage and daring. Firefighting is a team effort; if one firefighter fails to properly do his or her job, injury or death could occur. We depend on each other for our lives while protecting the life and property of the people of the city.

So, why become a firefighter?

- You will make friends for life
- You will appreciate clean, cool water after a hot fire
- You will enjoy warm clothing and dry feet
- You will have new respect for the sun and clean air
- You will make sure your loved ones are loved
- You will provide a safer environment for them

♦ You will know that basically all people are wonderful, with the same wants and needs

Society can sometimes be broken down into givers and takers. Firefighters are givers; they protect the lives and property of all people. They have even given their lives!

From the fire academy to college courses to lectures, the opportunity is there for anyone to learn the job and advance him- or herself by competitive promotional exams. The firefighter's uniform, both work and dress, is by far the most respected of all uniforms. It has a past, and a future, and a tradition. It means that firefighters give life. I am so proud to have worn that uniform!

Former New York Governor Mario Cuomo said it best when he praised New York City firefighters, calling them "the most heroic, finest people that ever inhabited New York." There is no finer tribute. And it's true of firefighters everywhere.

Bill Gates

CONTENTS

ABOUT THE AUTHOR

Mary Masi, M. A., is the founder of InfoSurge, a company specializing in writing, research, and editorial consulting. Previously, she worked in the editorial division of John Wiley & Sons, Inc., and before that, as a college English instructor.

ACKNOWLEDGMENTS

Grateful acknowledgment is made to the following individuals who contributed to the development of this book: William Gates, New York City Fire Captain, retired; Thomas Gates, New York City Firefighter, retired; and James Boyle, Director of the John Jay College Fire Institute in New York City and Retired President of the Uniformed Firefighter Association Local 94-AFL/CIO.

INTRODUCTION

WHY YOU NEED THIS BOOK

Firefighting today is a career that is highly sought after. Many job candidates are lining up to apply for each job opening in this competitive field. You can increase your chances of landing that highly-sought after job by reading this book and applying its principles to your job search. The book covers all the information you need to know about the many different aspects of the complicated application process for becoming a firefighter: the written exam, the physical ability exam, the oral interview, and more.

There are currently approximately 300,000 individuals employed as full-time paid firefighters (also called *career firefighters*) and close to one million volunteer firefighters. This exciting and demanding field is expected to grow through the year 2005 as a result of increased population and that populations' fire protection needs. However, competition for the available jobs is keen, so you can benefit by getting armed with the inside information and advice from current firefighters that fill this book.

Although the minimum requirements for becoming a firefighter in most cities and states across the country are a high school diploma or GED and excellent physical health, many prospective firefighters are going well beyond these requirements to enhance their chances for employment. Therefore, you need to be prepared to compete with candidates who have completed training courses—this book shows you how to find and enroll in training programs near you (and how to finance that training!). A whole range of fire-related careers are available to you, and this book gives you the inside information you need to select the fire services training program and career that's right for you.

In chapter one, you'll get an inside look at what the best opportunities are in firefighting today—from municipal firefighter to fire inspector to federal, state, and private job opportunities. This chapter contains useful information such as specific job descriptions, typical salaries, typical minimum requirements, trends in educational background, and fast-growing geographic locations. You'll find helpful advice from firefighting professionals from across the country who can give you the inside scoop on how to get hired. Use the checklist at the end of the chapter to verify that firefighting is indeed the career for you.

Chapter two shows you how to land the job you want. You'll find detailed information on how to succeed in the application process for a range of firefighting positions including how to prepare for the written and physical exams and how to ace the oral interviews and oral boards. How to use the Internet in your job search is clearly explained and several great Web sites are listed for your immediate use. A special section is included to give tips to people who are leaving the military and who want to enter the firefighting field.

In chapter three, you'll see how to select and evaluate training programs near you. You'll find sample courses that are taught in actual fire science training programs from different colleges and universities. These course descriptions can help you decide what training program is right for you and how long you need to go to school for each one. You'll also find a directory of fire science training programs that will give you a representative listing of schools across the country in order by city and state. So if you're considering moving to a new city, you can check that city's programs too. All programs provide names, addresses, and phone numbers so you can contact each school directly to get more information and application forms.

After you've selected a training program that's right for you, you'll find out how you can use financial aid to help you pay for it in chapter four. The chapter clearly explains the financial aid process step-by-step, so you can be prepared and get your aid as soon as possible. Several helpful checklists and tables are included for your use.

Once you've completed your training program and landed your first job, chapter five shows you how to succeed on that job. You'll find out what qualities are rewarded, how to move up in the ranks, and what specific advancement opportunities are available within the fire services field. You'll also find out what other career options and areas of specialization are available to you as you progress down your career path.

So read on to find out how you can land a job as a firefighter and succeed in this exciting, demanding, and heroic career.

CHAPTER | 1

Here's a thorough report on the latest trends in the fire-fighting field. The benefits of becoming a firefighter are clearly explained, as well as the emerging educational trends of prospective fire-fighters around the country. You'll get job descriptions and typical job require-ments and salaries for the following entry-level positions: municipal and volunteer firefighters, state and federal wildland firefighters, military and private company firefighters, EMT firefighters, fire inspec-tors, and fire protection engineers. Find out if fire-fighting is the career for you by taking the quiz at the end of the chapter.

FIREFIGHTING TODAY

The nature of firefighting is becoming more complex all the time. The days are gone when firefighters only responded to fires. More of today's firefighters are becoming certified as emergency medical technicians (EMTs) or paramedics than ever before to meet the increasing need for such services. Many calls to the firehouse require emergency procedures unrelated to fires, such as providing help to a heart attack victim or someone who is trapped under a structure or in a well. Fire-fighters also respond to vehicle accidents and fires, terrorist attacks, earthquakes, hurricanes and other natural disasters, and many miscellaneous 911 emergency calls. Therefore, firefighters need a broad range of skills, and they need to continually update their skills in additional training programs. As new technologies and equipment are created and additional emergencies and disasters arise, the demands on firefighters will become increasingly complex. However, along with all those demands come many benefits that firefighters receive while in the line of duty.

BENEFITS OF BECOMING A FIREFIGHTER

Many people are attracted to the firefighting field, but not all for the same reasons. There are several benefits to having a career in firefighting, as shown below. See what benefits appeal to you the most.

Work Schedule

Many people are drawn to firefighting because they do not want to sit behind a desk in an office job and work 9 to 5 for five days a week. The variety of the firefighter's work schedule appeals to people who want flexibility and large chunks of time off from work. Of course work schedules vary from department to department, but commonly firefighters work for 24 hours on duty followed by 48 or even 72 hours off duty or some other arrangement of significant time on and time off the job. Some firefighters use their days off to work outside jobs or conduct other business as a side income to supplement their firefighting salary. The average number of hours firefighters work each week is in the range of about 42-52. Some of those hours, however, are usually spent eating and sleeping in the firehouse.

In large urban fire departments, each shift may be shorter, such as 8 to 14 hours, depending on if it's a day, night, or weekend shift. Even with shorter shifts and more routine work schedules, firefighters on these shifts still have a large variety of tasks, and they never know what the next fire call will bring. While on duty, firefighters in less-busy departments may have free time after the maintenance and training for their shift is finished to visit and relax until the next call comes in.

The Lure of Adventure

While firefighting is dangerous and demanding work, several people say they joined the profession because they enjoy the excitement and rush of adrenaline that accompany fire calls. Some firefighters jump out of airplanes to fight wildland fires and others scout out dangerous areas inside structures. Many firefighters save people's lives and property on a regular basis. They face danger or unknown conditions every time they go out on an emergency call. People with adventurous and courageous spirits and a thirst for excitement are often drawn into firefighting.

Teamwork and Family Atmosphere

Since firefighters live and work so closely with each other, they often develop close bonds with one another. Teamwork is essential in fighting fires and is emphasized from day one in all training programs. This teamwork provides a secure atmosphere for all the members of the team. Firefighters spend a lot of time with each other when on long shifts at the firehouse—they often cook and eat large family-style meals around a big table and play cards or tell jokes during the wee hours of the morning when not out on calls. They sit in training courses together, and they test their skills by performing drills in friendly competition with each other. Kevin Scarbrough of the Ann Arbor, Michigan Fire Department says firefighters sometimes play practical jokes on each other while in the firehouse to help relieve the build-up of tension from the underlying feeling of danger that accompanies most fire calls, as well as to "test" how that person will react to the group when in a fire situation.

Positive Public Perception

Although not all firefighters will admit it, most enjoy being perceived as "heroes" by the public. Many children look up to firefighters with awe and respect when firefighters visit their schools for education programs. Just look at how many children go through a time of wanting to be a firefighter when they grow up. Even among adults, firefighters are often treated with a great deal of respect due to the dangerous and heroic nature of their jobs. Not only do they save people's lives and property, but they also provide emergency assistance in natural disasters and other times of calamity.

Health, Life, and Disability Insurance Benefits

Firefighters usually have a choice of health plans to select from their employer. These plans normally cover the firefighter and his or her dependents. Life and disability insurance are also provided due to the dangerous nature of the job. If firefighters are injured on the job, they can either get disability payments or retire early depending on the nature of the injury and the department's guidelines. Indeed, most states require that all local fire departments offer disability retirement benefits to their firefighters.

Retirement Benefits

Firefighters normally receive excellent retirement benefits. Due to the arduous nature of the job, many firefighters retire as soon as they reach the eligible age or time in the job. For example, some firefighters need to work for 25 years or until they are 55 years old, whichever comes earlier. So if you became a firefighter when you were 20 years old, you could retire at age 45 if your department had a 25-years-of-service rule. However, if your department required you to work until you were 55, then you would need to stay the additional 10 years. If you work for a municipal fire department, the local government agency employing you will set aside a certain amount of money for your retirement above and beyond what you contribute to your pension. Just ask one of the many retired firefighters living in Florida if they like their pension plan!

Good Salary

The earnings of most firefighters are relatively high compared to other jobs with a similar amount of training. Usually entry-level firefighters can earn a significant salary, which then increases with experience and additional training. Most fire departments offer firefighters longevity pay after they've served a number of years (ranging from 1 year in Brownsville, Texas to 22 years in Stockton, California). Longevity pay is a set amount added to firefighters' base salary every year after they become eligible to receive it. A typical amount of longevity pay is around $1,000 annually. For recent salary information for municipal career firefighters, see the Typical Salaries chart in the section entitled *Municipal Firefighter* shown later in this chapter. Many firefighters are also offered voluntary overtime on a rotating basis. Some firefighters jump at the chance for overtime pay, but others consistently refuse it due to family or other obligations. Fire departments may occasionally require mandatory overtime from their firefighters.

Access to a Union

Many firefighters belong to a union, either on a national or local level. These unions represent the needs of their members. The largest firefighter's labor organization in the country is called the International Association of Fire Fighters (IAFF) and has approximately 215,000 members. Some states have their own organizations—in California, the California State Firefighter's Association (CSFA) has been around for over 70 years and boasts over 28,000 members. The CSFA uses its resources to negotiate better wages and benefits and fair personnel policies for their members.

Miscellaneous Benefits

Other benefits that are commonly given to municipal firefighters include paid vacations, holidays, and sick time; a uniform allowance to pay for laundry and purchase of new uniforms; free training programs and tuition assistance for college and university fire studies; a free annual medical examination; and sometimes physical conditioning training and equipment to work on.

EDUCATIONAL TRENDS

While the published entrance requirements are minimal for becoming a municipal career firefighter, more and more applicants are gaining training and certification to boost their chances of getting hired. Years ago, firefighters could easily get hired with only the minimum requirements (having a high school diploma and being at least 18 years of age). However, nowadays, serious applicants are taking advantage of as many training programs as possible because there is such keen competition for jobs. Many prospective firefighters enroll in fire science certificate or associate degree programs or take specific courses such as Fire Hose and Fire Streams, Fire Behavior, Fire Tools and Equipment, and other fire-related courses to attain basic firefighting skills. Other prospective firefighters also complete Associate of Science degrees or obtain certificates from local colleges in Emergency Medical Technology (EMT) to increase their chances of landing a firefighting job.

If you are competing for jobs with people who have additional training under their belts, you'd be advised to seek some of this training yourself to keep in the running. Ask around to see what level of training and experience other prospective applicants have obtained. If you are in a medium to large city, chances are that some other applicants have or are attaining EMT, paramedic, or fire science training. See chapter 3 for more detailed information about the types of training programs that are available and how you can choose the one that's best for you.

FAST-GROWING GEOGRAPHIC LOCATIONS

If you don't mind relocating in your quest for a career firefighter position, there are areas of the country that employ larger numbers of firefighters than others. According to a recruitment specialist at a major firefighting and EMS recruiting firm, the fastest-growing geographic locations are along the west coast. He cites growth in the states of California, Arizona, and Colorado as well as the southern states of Georgia and Florida but notes that hiring is a bit slow in the New England states. By taking advantage of the openings in the growing areas of the country, you can increase your chances of getting hired.

WHO EMPLOYS FIREFIGHTERS?

Roughly 300,000 career firefighters are employed nationwide as paid, full-time professionals. So who hires all these career firefighters? Well, if you're in the majority—nine out of 10, according to the Bureau of Labor Statistics (BLS)—you'll be employed by a municipal or county fire department, typically serving a community with a population of 50,000 or more. Not surprisingly, large cities are the largest employers.

Full-time firefighters are also hired by federal and state government agencies to protect government-owned property and special facilities. For example, the U.S. Forest Service, Bureau of Land Management, and Park Service offer both year-round and seasonal fire service jobs to protect the country's national parks, forests, and other lands.

In the private sector, many large industrial companies have their own fire-fighting forces, especially companies in the oil, chemical, aircraft, and aerospace industries. Other employers include airports, shipyards, and military bases. Also, a growing number of private companies are in the business of providing fire protection services—including on-call or on-site firefighting teams—to other businesses and institutions.

In addition to career firefighters, there are close to a million volunteer or "paid-call" firefighters nationwide. These individuals work mostly in rural or small communities and may receive compensation only when they are called to duty, or they may receive no monetary compensation at all but get free training and a uniform allowance.

JOB OPPORTUNITIES IN THE FIRE PROTECTION FIELD

Many people are needed to fight fires—both on the front lines and in the background. While the majority of firefighters work for municipal fire departments, there are also jobs available in the private sector, in the military, and for state and federal governments. Several opportunities exist for volunteer firefighters in many locations across the country. In addition to these front-line positions, there are other jobs that take place more in the background. For example, there are some fire-related jobs that focus on events and building codes before a fire ever takes place: fire protection engineers, and fire inspectors.

Listed below are several different entry-level job opportunities in the firefighting field for you to consider. Look closely at the job description, typical minimum requirements needed, and typical salaries for each job to help make your decision of where in the fire service you want to build a career.

FIRE SUPPRESSION
Municipal Firefighter

Nine out of 10 firefighters work for municipal (local government) fire departments. Since this is the most common job in the firefighting field, it's the one you've probably heard the most about. These are the firefighters who are paid, full-time workers (also called *career firefighters* to distinguish them from volunteer or part-time firefighters). They fight fires and respond to emergency situations within their local community, and once in awhile they may be called by other surrounding fire departments to offer mutual aid for extremely serious fires.

Municipal firefighters work in teams and are assigned specific tasks to ensure optimal organization at the scene of a fire. Most fire departments have a combination of one or more of the following: engine company, ladder company, pump company, and truck company. Firefighters are assigned to one of these "companies" within the fire department, so they know exactly what they need to focus on when the next fire call comes in. Some firefighters become apparatus operators (also known as firetruck drivers) after serving as firefighters for some time and passing a promotional exam, some firefighters are assigned pump duty, others enter the burning structure, others handle the ladders, and some firefighters are busy venting the roof. Every fire call is different, but firefighters all work together in an organized and systematic way by following orders according to the chain of command. Their leader may be the fire chief, the assistant fire chief, the captain, or a person with some other title, depending on the size and location of the fire department.

There are several levels of rank for firefighters in municipal departments, and many opportunities for promotion and advancement, depending on the size and location of the department. Most fire departments have a combination of the following job titles and ranks:

Firefighter Recruit

Firefighter Level I

Firefighter Level II

Apparatus Operator (Truck Driver)

Fire Lieutenant

Fire Captain

Battalion Chief

District Chief

Deputy Chief

Assistant Fire Chief

Fire Chief

After completing the application process for a municipal firefighting position, applicants are rated and placed on an eligibility list. If you are called from this list, and you pass all subsequent tests and interviews and are hired, you'll need to complete a training program to find out the specific requirements of the department that hired you. You'll be called a probationary firefighter (known as *probie* to insiders) for the first 6 to 18 months, depending on the length of probation required in your area. See chapter 5 for information about advancement opportunities within municipal fire departments.

Typical Minimum Requirements

While requirements vary, most municipal fire departments require applicants to have the minimum of a high school diploma or General Equivalency Diploma (G.E.D.), be at least 18 years old, and pass a physical ability exam. Some states require that state certification be obtained by prospective firefighters before they are considered for a job. Since there is such intense competition for job openings, however, many applicants go well above and beyond the minimum requirements by getting volunteer firefighting experience and specialized training from a college fire science program to gain an edge on the competition. See chapter 3 for a list of fire science training programs in your area.

Typical Salaries

While salaries vary greatly depending on the location and availability of funds in each fire department, most firefighters enjoy a relatively high salary, especially as they advance and attain higher levels of training. See the table below for firefighter salaries in a range of locations to get an idea of what you can expect. You can also look in the annual publication entitled *Municipal Year Book*, found in the reference department of your local public library, for recent salary information for municipal firefighters.

Location	Annual Salary Range
Baton Rouge, Louisiana	$17,341-$25,465
Fayettville, Arkansas	$20,948-$28,770
Birmingham, Alabama	$22,854-$32,188
Austin, Texas	$23,868-$44,184
Columbus, Ohio	$24,103-$36,712
Atlanta, Georgia	$25,498-$36,426
Jersey City, New Jersey	$26,320-53,676
Fort Worth, Texas	$28,800-$35,007
New York, New York	$29,100-$43,593
Detroit, Michigan	$29,551-$39,033
Albany, New York	$32,857-$40,853
Rochester, Minnesota	$34,587-$46,094
Oakland, California	$48,456-$53,472

Volunteer or Paid-Call Firefighter

There are approximately 1 million volunteer firefighters in the U.S. today. Many prospective career firefighters become volunteer firefighters so they can gain experience and use their skills as they conduct their job search or wait for their number to be called from eligibility lists of paid departments. There is an increasing time commitment required by many volunteer fire departments, so the demands are great without any or with very little pay. Volunteer firefighters often do not receive any monetary compensation for their work, but paid-call firefighters usually receive minimum wage, or a similar level of earnings for each fire call that they go on. Therefore, paid-call firefighting positions are similar to volunteer, but they do offer nominal compensation. Even with little or no pay, many firefighters regularly give their time to volunteer departments and pursue certification and additional training to gain experience for a paid career firefighting position.

Volunteers may serve with career firefighters in the same fire company, or they may comprise an entire fire company, with only a paid fire chief and assistant who work full-time for the department. Some volunteer firefighters are given pagers, so they don't have to spend so much time in the fire station waiting for fire calls. If they are on-call and their pager goes off, they put a blue light/siren in the window of their car and rush to the fire station to get on the fire truck and head to the fire. Volunteer firefighters who are properly certified can perform the same functions that paid career firefighters do.

The experience you receive as a volunteer firefighter can be different depending on the type of crew you work with. If you become a volunteer who works with a full crew of paid career firefighters, you can get an inside look at how things are run in the firehouse and at fires by a municipal department. You normally have to put in a certain number of hours at the firehouse, instead of getting a pager and going on-call outside of the firehouse. However, there can be some adjustment needed to fit in with the career firefighters when you are the only volunteer on duty. Therefore, you might want to look for a firefighting crew that is made up of all volunteers to get more of a feeling of camaraderie.

Typical Minimum Requirements

While minimum requirements vary among fire departments, volunteer firefighters normally have to undergo some type of training before they can begin work and further training before they can enter a burning building. Some counties and states require all volunteers to become certified before beginning to work. Jeffrey Cuttitta, a volunteer firefighter in Long Island, New York, said he went through several procedures before being selected to serve: a physical exam, 10 weeks of classroom and 10 weeks of hands-on training, waiting for an opening to occur, and getting sworn in. After joining the department, he became a *probie*, which is a firefighter on probation. He then had to pass a written and physical exam, attend all meetings and drills, and go to a certain percentage of fire calls for one year to get off of probation status. He did, and then he went on to attain Firefighter I certification from the local fire academy after significant training.

All volunteer programs are different however, so you may find that you only need to sign up and take a physical exam before being sworn in as a volunteer or paid-call firefighter in a small fire company.

Typical Salaries

While volunteer firefighters usually don't get paid, there are several benefits to becoming a volunteer firefighter: gaining firefighting experience, getting to know career firefighters, and learning to work as a team. Some volunteers do get small allowances to pay for their transportation to and from the fire department, and paid-call firefighters usually get minimum wage or a similar level of pay for each hour they spend on a fire call.

State Wildland Firefighter

Many state government agencies hire firefighters to protect state-owned land. Every year, state agencies that are responsible for state lands have to deal with the threat of wildfires—fast-spreading burns that can scorch thousands and thousands of acres. These fires are often in remote regions with limited access, which makes fighting them perilous and brutal work. Fires on this scale are not controlled merely by using fire hoses, but by limiting where and how much the fire burns. The states that employ the most firefighters are located in the western portion of the U. S., since these states have the most forests or wildlands in them. However, other states employ limited number of state firefighters too. For example, in Minnesota, the Department of Natural Resources (DNR) has two divisions that hire seasonal firefighters: the forestry division and the state park division.

Most entry-level state firefighters are hired only during the season that most fires occur—and that fire season is different depending on the state. Arizona, for instance, often employs firefighters from March to July (the monsoons arrive in July) and then again in October if it's a dry year. On the other hand, California often doesn't hire until May, but their season can last until December. Seasonal wildland firefighting is quite a bit different from structural firefighting due to the nature and location of the fire. Much of the work is hard manual labor, such as cutting down brush and trees that are in the way of the fire. Excellent physical condition is required to keep up the pace of hard work for several days in a row as the fire rages since most wildland fires last much longer than structural fires.

At the state level, the California Department of Forestry calls itself the largest fire department in the country because it employs from 2,500 to 3,500 firefighters every fire season. The state posts its openings for firefighters each year, and in 1996 more than 10,000 applications were received—so it's highly competitive! The filing deadline is usually in January or early February, and if you miss it, you'll have to wait until the following year to sign up. Many states, though, such as those in the southeast, often find themselves running short of personnel, particularly during the peak of the fire season.

Typical Minimum Requirements

Excellent physical condition is required for wildland firefighters due to the heavy manual labor, harsh conditions, and longevity and intensity of wildland fires. Of course, a good work record will increase your chances of getting hired, even if it's in an unrelated field. You must be at least 18 years old and possess a high school diploma or its equivalent. Any additional specific requirements vary from state to state.

Typical Salaries

The salaries are normally lower for entry-level state firefighters than they are for entry-level municipal firefighters, and the work is seasonal rather than all year round. The pay normally ranges from $8.30 to $10.00 per hour, but many firefighters get significantly more by adding overtime and hazard (actual frontline fighting) pay to their base pay. Also, firefighters who live in communities that have a high cost of living may receive higher wages.

Federal Firefighter

Various departments of the federal government employ firefighters for a variety of programs. The two most common programs are discussed below.

Wildland Firefighter

This job is similar to the one mentioned above that is on the state level—fighting fires in the wildlands or in forests—only this job is to fight fires that occur on federal lands and in federal parks rather than on state lands and parks. The fires these firefighters fight are caused both by human and natural forces: the campfire that went awry or a bolt of lightning that hit dry brush. Similar to state firefighters, federal firefighters also must engage in hard physical labor to stop raging forest or wildland fires.

For example, crews will be rushed into an area that is threatened and told to "scrape it down to mineral." This means that all the vegetation—dried grass, plants, dead wood, and anything else that would burn—has to be scraped clean to the dirt. Essentially, the crews are trying to stop the fire by cutting back its fuel. In the wilds, this work could involve a four-person crew scraping an eight-foot wide path for two miles. And doing it fast—in hot, dry conditions—as the front of the fire approaches. Other tactics include starting and controlling a small fire and guiding it toward the front of the original fire to take away its fuel.

Large, raging wildland or forest fires can be like wars—firefighting crews are flown and trucked in, air tankers are coordinated with the ground troops, support crews providing food, medical, and mail services converge on the scene. The shifts for firefighters can run 16-24 hours or more of hard physical labor in heavy gear as the air temperature often exceeds 100 degrees, which is why you need to be in excellent physical shape.

There are various levels and duties for federal firefighters. The first step is usually to work for a national forest, becoming a general wildland firefighter (referred to as a type-two firefighter) who works to support the front-line firefighting crew (called type-one firefighters). The next move up would be to join an engine company, then work your way up to joining a type-one crew, the members of which are called *hot shots* and who fight at the front line of the fire. Finally, you can apply to become a *smoke jumper*. There are currently approximately 2,200 firefighters who work as part of a *hot shot* type-one team and about 360 smoke jumpers nationwide, with several thousand type-two firefighters—those who are not on the front-lines. Timo Rova, a smoke jumper who works out of Montana, explains the exciting role of a *smoke jumper*.

> Smoke jumpers parachute out of airplanes to fight fires where no ground access is available. We carry heavy packs of supplies and stay out on the fire for up to three days before new provisions are dropped in to us or we leave the area. Sometimes we end up walking out after we control the fire and it might be a 16 mile trek back to the ground crew headquarters. Other times, we get a lift out on a helicopter, but overall, it is very demanding work. We need to pass physical tests every year to maintain smoke jumper status.

Many federal firefighters are flown to different states to fight fires in a variety of locations throughout the fire season, depending on need and weather patterns. The branches of the federal government that hire the most firefighters are the U. S. Park Service, the U. S. Forest Service, and the Bureau of Land Management. See Appendix A to obtain their addresses.

Typical Minimum Requirements

Standards vary among the different branches of the federal government, but in general, applicants need to be physically strong, be at least 18 years old, and have a high school diploma or its equivalent. An example of a physical test you might need to pass is as follows: be able to do 7 pull-ups, 25 push-ups, 45 sit-ups, run 1 1/2 miles in 11 minutes or less, and carry a 110-pound pack 3 miles—all in under 90 minutes. Those are the physical requirements of one federal agency for landing a job as a smoke jumper.

Typical Salaries

The salaries for entry-level federal firefighters start at about $8.30 per hour but many firefighters get significantly more by adding overtime and hazard pay to their base. Also, after you've been a federal firefighter for a few years, you can expect to earn more. A federal firefighter from Minnesota with over five years of experience earned $12.00 an hour in 1997. However, some years he was able to make as much as $26,000 during one fire season, due to extensive overtime and hazard pay. The salaries for seasonal federal firefighters can vary greatly depending on the length and severity of the fire season.

Military Firefighters

Another branch of the federal government that employs firefighters is the Department of Defense. There are a range of opportunities within the Department of Defense for various types of firefighting. Military bases need fire protection, just like rural or urban communities. The main difference is that military bases employ people who are enlisted in the military and other federal employees to become base firefighters instead of relying on the local municipal fire department.

Since the job duties of a military firefighter are similar to those of a municipal firefighter's, the job offers good experience to someone who wants to apply for a municipal firefighting job upon completion of the military service. Approximately 2,200 firefighters are employed by the military, and approximately 350 new firefighters are needed each year. While all branches of the military employ firefighters, the two branches of the military that train and employ the most firefighters are the air force and the navy.

Air Force

The air force trains firefighters in how to protect aircrafts when accidents occur during take-offs and landings as well as how to fight structural fires and deal with hazardous materials. The air force offers a thirteen-week fire academy training course at the Goodfellow Air Force Base in San Angelo, Texas in how to fight fires and how to use firefighting equipment for a variety of needs. The air force gives firefighters training on a regular basis and their training courses offer students college credit from the Community College of the Air Force. Therefore, many air force firefighters can obtain an Associate degree through this on-going training.

Most air force bases employ a mix of military members and federal civilians. Since military members are often moved around to different bases depending on need, the civilian firefighters remain at the same base to maintain a sense of continuity. The civilian firefighters on military air force bases are employed by the federal government. According to Floyd Virgil, a military firefighter at the Keesler Air Force Base, several federal civilian firefighters were previously military firefighters, so they have experience when they apply for the job of civilian firefighter at a military base. He also believes that military firefighters have a good chance of getting hired outside the military because it's known that the military has very rigorous and up-to-date fire service training programs.

When you talk to air force recruiters, you need to ask them if you can get a guarantee of being trained and placed in the fire protection field of the air force. If you achieve a high enough score on the skills tests and pass all other requirements, the air force may guarantee in writing that your career area will be within the fire protection field as a part of your enlistment agreement. After you enlist with the air force, you'll undergo basic training at Lackland Air Force Base in San Antonio, Texas for six weeks. If you have fire protection guaranteed as your career area, you'll then be sent to the Goodfellow Air Force Base in San Angelo, Texas for the thirteen-week training program before being assigned to a fire department. Air Force enlistment periods are for either four or six years.

Navy

The navy, as one might imagine, offers training to firefighters on how to combat fire on its fleet of ships, as well as other related operations. This type of firefighting is often called *damage control* within the navy. You can also check into getting a job as a part of the aircraft fire rescue team in the navy for aircrafts that crash into the water. The navy offers certified apprenticeship programs for some specialties within the firefighting occupation.

The growth of firefighting visibility in the navy is evidenced by the establishment of a new award in 1994, called the Homer W. Carhart Award for Fire Protection Excellence. Dr. Homer W. Carhart is a Senior Scientist Emeritus at the Naval Research Laboratory (NRL) in Washington, DC. He is an expert in the areas of safety, fire protection, and shipboard survivability, with over 50 years of experience in these areas. The award was established by the Chief of Naval Operations to recognize superior achievement in the areas of safety and shipboard survivability excellence.

Basic training for the navy is conducted in Great Lakes, Illinois and lasts for eight weeks and three days. You can choose to enlist in the navy for a time period of three, four, five, or six years.

Typical Minimum Requirements

First of all, you need the minimum requirements for joining the military. These are: you must be 17 years of age or older, a U. S. citizen or legal immigrant alien, in good health, drug free, and have a clean arrest record. Then, to become a firefighter in the military, you need to achieve an acceptable score on the Armed Services Vocational Aptitude Battery (ASVAB) prior to enlisting. At this printing, applicants need to achieve a score of 39 in the general category and be in excellent physical condition to be admitted to the fire protection career area. You also need to pass a medical exam before being admitted to the military.

Typical Salaries

Salaries for firefighters in the military are on the same scale as for other military jobs. The salary depends on the years of experience and the grade level or rank you have obtained. See the table below for a range of salaries in the military. The dollar amounts in the table combine basic pay, the basic allowance for quarters, the basic allowance for subsistence, and the average variable housing allowance. They also include the tax advantage from untaxed allowances. The figures do not include the average overseas housing allowance or the overseas cost-of-living allowance.

1997 military base pay chart

Years of Service

Grade	<2	2	3	4	6	8	10	12	14	16	18	20	22	24	26
Commissioned officers															
O-10	7360.20	7619.10	7619.10	7619.10	7619.10	7911.60	7911.60	8349.90	8349.90	8947.20	8947.20	9546.30	9546.30	9546.30	10140.90
O-9	6522.90	6693.90	6836.70	6836.70	6836.70	7010.40	7010.40	7302.00	7302.00	7911.60	7911.60	8349.90	8349.90	8349.90	8947.20
O-8	5908.20	6085.50	6229.80	6229.80	6229.80	6693.90	6692.90	7010.40	7010.40	7302.00	7619.10	7911.60	8106.60	8106.60	8106.60
O-7	4909.20	5243.10	5243.10	5243.10	5478.30	5478.30	5785.70	6080.70	6080.70	6863.90	7154.40	7154.40	7154.40	7154.40	7154.40
O-6	3638.40	3997.50	4259.70	4259.70	4259.70	4259.70	4259.70	4259.70	4404.60	5100.90	4809.60	5478.30	5795.70	5991.60	6285.60
O-5	2913.30	3417.00	3653.40	3653.40	3653.40	3653.40	3763.50	3853.50	4232.90	4549.20	4809.60	4955.70	5128.80	5128.80	5128.80
O-4	2452.80	2987.10	3186.30	3186.30	3245.40	3388.50	3619.80	3823.20	3997.50	4173.30	4287.90	4287.90	4287.90	4287.90	4287.90
O-3	2279.40	2548.50	2722.90	3014.70	3159.00	3272.10	3449.40	3619.80	3708.60	3708.60	3708.60	3708.60	3708.60	3708.60	3708.60
O-2	1987.80	2178.80	2608.20	2695.80	2751.60	2751.60	2751.60	2751.60	2751.60	2751.60	2751.60	2751.60	2751.60	2751.60	2751.60
O-1	1725.50	1796.10	2170.80	2170.80	2170.80	2170.80	2170.80	2170.80	2170.80	2107.50	2170.80	2170.80	2170.80	2170.80	2170.80
Officers with more than 4 years active duty as enlisted or warrant officer															
O-3E	0.00	0.00	0.00	3014.70	3159.00	3272.10	3449.40	3619.80	3763.50	3763.50	3763.50	3763.50	3763.50	3763.50	3763.50
O-2E	0.00	0.00	0.00	2695.80	2751.60	2695.60	2695.80	3107.40	3186.30	3186.30	3186.30	3186.30	3186.30	3186.30	3186.30
O-1E	0.00	0.00	0.00	2170.80	2319.30	2404.50	2491.80	2578.20	2695.80	2695.80	2695.80	2695.80	2695.80	2695.80	2695.80
Warrant officers															
W-5	0.00	0.00	0.00	0.00	0.00	0.00	0.00	0.00	0.00	0.00	0.00	3933.60	4113.60	4232.70	4410.60
W-4	2322.30	2491.80	2491.80	2548.50	2664.60	2781.90	2896.60	3101.40	3245.40	3359.40	3449.40	3560.70	3679.80	3794.40	3966.60
W-3	2110.80	2289.60	2289.60	2319.30	2346.30	2317.80	2695.60	2751.60	3186.60	3014.70	3132.30	2724.90	2923.80	2923.80	2923.80
W-2	1848.60	2000.10	2000.10	2058.30	2170.80	2289.60	2376.60	2463.60	2548.50	2638.20	2724.90	2810.40	2923.80	2923.80	2923.80
W-1	1540.20	1765.80	1765.80	1913.40	2000.10	2003.90	2176.20	2293.20	2348.30	2433.30	2548.30	2608.20	2695.20	2695.20	2695.20
Enlisted members															
E-9	0.00	0.00	0.00	0.00	0.00	0.00	2701.80	2762.40	2824.80	2889.90	2954.70	3011.70	3169.80	3293.40	3478.50
E-8	0.00	0.00	0.00	0.00	0.00	2255.60	2310.70	2389.70	2451.10	2519.10	2724.90	2802.70	2724.90	2209.30	3102.60
E-7	1581.90	1707.90	1770.60	1833.00	1895.40	1955.70	2018.40	2081.40	2175.30	2237.10	2298.90	2329.20	2485.50	2609.10	2794.80
E-6	1360.80	1485.50	1545.00	1603.50	1671.00	1731.30	1794.00	1857.30	1887.30	1924.80	1924.00	2349.00	2349.00	2349.00	2349.00
E-5	1194.30	1299.90	1362.90	1422.30	1515.90	1577.70	1639.80	1700.40	1731.30	1731.30	1731.30	1731.30	1731.30	1731.30	1731.30
E-4	1113.00	1175.30	1241.80	1241.80	1241.80	1241.80	1241.80	1241.80	1241.80	1241.80	1241.80	1241.80	1241.80	1241.80	1241.80
E-3	1049.70	1107.00	1151.10	1196.70	1196.70	1196.70	1196.70	1196.70	1196.70	1196.70	1196.70	1196.70	1196.70	1196.70	1196.70
E-2	1010.10	1010.10	1010.10	1010.10	1010.10	1010.10	1010.10	1010.10	1010.10	1010.10	1010.10	1010.10	1010.10	1010.10	1010.10
E-1>4	900.90	900.90	900.90	900.90	900.90	900.90	900.90	900.90	900.90	900.90	900.90	900.90	900.90	900.90	900.90
E-1 with less than 4 months	832.40														

Note: Basic pay is limited to $9016.80 per month. Figures for O-10 in the chart show what pay would be without the cap.

Firefighters in Private Companies

In addition to the many job opportunities offered by government agencies, there are firefighting jobs available from private companies. You can look for jobs from the following types of businesses:

- Oil and Chemical Refineries
- Large corporations
- Airports
- Shipyards

A majority of the private-sector jobs for firefighters can be found in companies in the petrochemical, aircraft, and aerospace industries, such as Boeing. Many private firefighters become highly specialized by focusing their training and inspection activities to one location and the major threat in that area, such as oil fires in an oil company or airplane fires in an airport.

A growing trend is for private firefighting companies to set up shop to provide firefighters to various companies, sometimes along with additional fire prevention and protection services. One private company that does this is Rural/Metro Corporation, which currently provides fire protection services to more than 25 communities and responds to more than 60,000 calls annually. They are based in Arizona, but they have offices across the nation.

Typical Minimum Requirements

Of course, the minimum requirements needed for each private company will vary somewhat. In general, applicants should be in good physical condition and have solid work experience to get the best opportunities for firefighting jobs in the private sector. Some specialized training could also prove quite useful, such as hazardous materials certification for applying to oil and chemical companies. Many private firefighting companies have a selection process that is similar to municipal fire departments and require thorough written and physical testing and some form of fire service training before hiring applicants.

Typical Salaries

Salaries vary among the different private fire companies, just as they do in other private industries. However, most private companies will have salaries similar to municipal firefighting departments in order to recruit high-quality applicants.

EMT Firefighters

Firefighter EMTs (known as Emergency Medical Technicians or Paramedics) are trained to provide emergency medical care, including ambulance services. They respond to a variety of emergency situations as well as fires. For example, they assist victims of natural disasters and spills of hazardous materials, as well as other medical emergencies, such as heart attack, stroke, and choking victims. They assess, manage, and administer treatment to ill or injured persons on the way to hospitals or other medical facilities, most often in a life-support unit or an ambulance. EMTs rely on radio communication to transmit information about a patient's condition and to receive medical instruction from a physician or other medical professional. The level of treatment they are allowed to provide depends on their level of training and certification.

Three levels of EMT certification are recognized by the National Registry of Emergency Medical Technicians: Basic, Intermediate, and Paramedic. Training programs are offered nationwide from colleges and universities; from hospitals; and from police, fire, and government health departments. Most EMT-Basic programs are modeled on a 110-hour standard training course developed by the U.S. Department of Transportation. Candidates must meet certain minimum requirements (for example, minimum age 18, high school diploma or GED, valid driver's license). Programs for EMT-Intermediate and EMT-Paramedic cover progressively more advanced levels of medical treatment and, of course, require completion of the prior level(s) of training.

Some fire departments are now requiring all new recruits to become certified as an EMT-Basic or EMT-Paramedic on a routine basis, instead of allowing firefighters to choose to specialize in this area. Large urban departments in particular are keen on EMT training due to the typically high level of responsibility they have for providing emergency medical services in the community.

Typical Minimum Requirements

To acquire EMT-Basic certification, you need to complete an approved training program, usually consisting of approximately 100 to 120 hours of study. EMT-Intermediate certification requires approximately 35 to 55 hours of additional instruction on top of the EMT-Basic training. EMT-Paramedic is the most advanced level of EMT training and requires approximately 750-2,000 hours of training in total (that includes the EMT-Basic and EMT-Intermediate hours of training). EMT-Paramedics often complete an Associate of Science degree in the course of their training.

Typical Salaries

According to a study published in 1995 in the *Journal of Emergency Medical Services*, EMT-Basic firefighters earn an average of $33,962, EMT-Intermediate firefighters earn an average of $35,667, and EMT-Paramedic firefighters earn an average of $37,690.

FIRE PREVENTION

Fire Inspector

Most fire inspectors deal with commercial or other non-residential structures. These structures account for only 9-10 percent of all fires, 5-6 percent of fire deaths, and 13-14 percent of injuries. Total deaths in non-residential structures are at a 10-year low. Fire Inspectors examine buildings to eliminate fire hazards and also to monitor fire protection equipment (such as sprinkler systems, extinguishers, and alarms) to ensure it is operable. Inspectors also patrol plant areas to determine if hazardous and combustible materials are stored properly. According to Kevin Scarbrough, an experienced fire inspector in Ann Arbor, Michigan, many inspectors focus on the new construction of buildings to ensure they meet all required state and local fire codes as they are being built. Some fire inspectors also offer fire education information to schools and local civic groups.

The job of fire inspector is held both by entry-level people who are trained in fire inspection procedures and by experienced firefighters who took promotions and gained additional training to land the position, depending on the organizational structure and size of the fire department. Historically, the fire inspector was a firefighter first and then learned the duties of fire inspection through promotion exams. The growing trend now, however, is for fire departments or fire prevention bureaus to hire entry-level fire inspectors who have specialized college-level training, but no firefighting experience.

Typical Minimum Requirements

The typical minimum requirements for becoming a fire inspector vary greatly, depending on the fire agency doing the hiring. In some fire departments, you would have to serve as a firefighter for several years (anywhere from 4 to 15 years or more) before an opening and a promotion opportunity would arise to become a fire inspector. In these departments, the length of time before getting a promotion to fire inspector depends on the department's needs. Other fire departments are opening up the position of fire inspector to graduates of fire science degree programs who haven't ever served as firefighters.

Typical Salaries

Salaries vary among departments and locations, but an average salary for a fire inspector in 1995 was $34,000. That figure includes both entry-level fire inspectors and long-term firefighters who were promoted to fire inspectors, so there is quite a variance in low to top pay. For those fire inspectors who have been firefighters for several years before landing the job of fire inspector, their salary range is quite high relative to entry-level fire inspectors.

Fire Protection Engineers

Fire protection engineers take advanced courses in mathematics, physics, and chemistry to gain scientific knowledge used in the research, design, installation, and operation of physical systems related to fire safety. Job opportunities in this arena far exceed the number of fire protection engineering graduates each year. They often work outside of fire departments, usually in the private sector. The majority of fire protection engineers do not begin their careers as firefighters.

Fire protection engineers can be called upon to provide a broad range of services. Some perform fire safety evaluations of building and industrial complexes to determine the risks of fire loss and to find the best ways to prevent fires. Others design systems that automatically detect and suppress fires and explosions as well as fire alarm, smoke control, emergency lighting, communication, and exit systems. Fire protection engineers perform research on materials and consumer products or on the computer modeling of fire and smoke behavior. Some investigate fires or explosions and prepare technical reports or provide expert courtroom testimony in civil litigation cases.

Many fire protection engineers are hired to oversee the design and operation of safety procedures for large companies. This area is of major concern to complex manufacturing facilities, such as refineries, chemical plants, and multinational business networks. These companies know that a million dollars spent in prevention and preparation can save tens of millions in clean-up costs and fines—not to mention the invaluable savings in terms of presenting a good image to the public.

Fire protection engineers also work for insurance companies, surveying major facilities and performing research, testing, and analysis. As the computer and electronics industry grows, its special needs of fire prevention expand as well. When a room full of high-tech gear is threatened by fire, the best course of action usually is not to turn on the water sprinklers. Finding new ways to prevent and suppress fires and save costly equipment is proving to be a new viable avenue for employment.

Fire protection engineers also work for architectural and engineering firms, automatic sprinkler companies, large hotel chains, and specialty consulting groups. Aside from private-sector companies, they can be found at all levels of government around the world. Other interesting jobs that use their expertise can be found in trade associations, testing laboratories, and at colleges and universities.

Typical Minimum Requirements

Fire protection engineers have a more advanced educational background than firefighters that typically includes a bachelor of science degree in a traditional engineering field or in fire science and often a master's degree in fire protection. Since the job demand for fire protection engineers far exceeds the number of qualified candidates, many companies actively recruit on the college campuses that offer fire protection engineering degrees.

Typical Salaries

Due to a great demand and to the high education level they obtain, fire protection engineers normally make more money than career firefighters. Their salaries are competitive in the industry and generally are higher than the average salary for the overall engineering profession, which ranges from $39,000-$50,000.

Firefighting Equipment

- boots and gloves
- helmet
- bunker pants and coat
- flashlight
- Swiss Army knife
- small rope
- chocks
- radio
- nomex hood
- compressed air scott mask

IS FIREFIGHTING THE RIGHT CAREER FOR YOU?

After reading the job descriptions listed above for a variety of entry-level fire-related positions, you are now ready to take the following tests to see if you are really cut out for a firefighting career and if so, what area would suit you best. You must be interested in the fire service field, or you wouldn't be reading this book. But are you sure you want to be a firefighter instead of a fire prevention specialist? Read on to find out!

Should You Become a Firefighter?

Find out if you really are suited to becoming a firefighter. Write down your answers to the following questions and then take a look at what those answers mean by reading the paragraph after the test.

1. Are you physically fit and do you have good upper body strength?
2. Do you enjoy working out and staying in shape?
3. Do you enjoy working in teams?
4. Do you like to get adrenaline rushes?
5. Do you prefer a flexible work schedule?
6. Do you enjoy enforcing rules?
7. Do you like to teach others?
8. Do you smoke cigarettes or cigars?
9. Do you enjoy a daily routine that is similar every day?
10. Do you value a high level of privacy and space at work?
11. Can you follow instructions properly and quickly?
12. Do you enjoy working outdoors?
13. Are you interested in learning about medical emergency technology?
14. Are you flexible and adaptable?
15. Can you think on your feet in situations of chaos and stress?
16. Do you prefer a regular work schedule that is the same every week?
17. Is working out and staying in shape a constant battle for you?
18. Are you afraid of heights or closed-in spaces?
19. Do you have a strong sense of independence?
20. Would you enjoy studying chemistry and physics?
21. Can you handle seeing gory and unpleasant things at work?
22. Are you willing to risk your life to save others?
23. Do you enjoy the thrill of adventure?
24. Do you enjoy experiencing new situations each day?
25. Do you like to play team sports?

If you answered *yes* to the majority of questions numbered 1-5, 11-15, and 21-25, then you'll probably want to go for a job in fire suppression. If you answered *yes* to the majority of questions numbered 6-10 and 16-20, then you'll probably want to go for a job in fire prevention or other fire-related services, not fire suppression. If you answered *yes* to all of the questions listed above, then you can take your pick of fire suppression or fire prevention/instruction because you appear to be well-suited for either career area. However, if you answered *no* to the majority of the questions above, then you might want to think about selecting another occupation altogether!

Who:	Lee R. Starrick
What:	Fire Lieutenant
Where:	Kennedy Space Center
How long:	Almost 30 years

Insider's Advice:

I've seen a lot of changes in the fire service over the years. I kind of fell into this job after spending time in the military as a firefighter. While the work schedule is good, 24 hours on followed by 48 hours off, and the pay is good, there are drawbacks to the job. For instance, firefighters have a very high divorce rate—now I don't know if that's because firefighters are not home enough, or if it's because they're home too much! Also, the family atmosphere and general camaraderie that the fire department used to have just isn't as strong as it used to be. For example, years ago, if one firefighter needed a roof put on his house, the whole crew would show up on our day off to help him put on the roof. You don't see that happening nowadays.

On the other hand, there is never a dull moment as a firefighter. A positive aspect of my job is the variety of the work we perform while on duty. One minute we might be supporting liquid oxygen and liquid hydrogen transfers at the launch pads, and the next we are fighting a structural or car fire. We support space shuttle landings and aircraft landings and take-offs at the runway. We also provide fire and rescue support for all shuttle launches and operations that take place at the space center. Our department includes water rescue, launch pad rescue, and hazardous materials teams.

Insider's Take on the Future:

I will retire very shortly—when my 30 years of service to the Kennedy Space Center are complete. While I enjoyed my firefighting career very much, I am looking forward to retirement.

CHAPTER | 2

This chapter gives you the information you need to come out a winner in the challenging process of landing a job as a firefighter in any of the following areas: municipal fire department, state or federal government, the military, or a private fire company. For municipal fire departments, who hire the most firefighters annually, you'll get inside tips on how to ace every portion of the formal application process: the physical ability test, the written exam, the oral interview, the oral board, and much more. You'll get the latest information on how you can use the Internet to land a job as well as how veteran's preference points can boost your application's score.

HOW TO LAND THE JOB YOU WANT

Now that you've decided that firefighting is the right career for you, how do you land a job in this exciting field? Well, competition for job openings is tough, so you need to arm yourself with the latest information to succeed in landing a job. Most fire departments put job applicants through a rigorous selection process that can take from several months to a year or more because they want to find firefighters who will excel on the job. Firefighters need to be smart enough to learn the chemistry, physics, and biology of emergency services; strong enough to carry a person out of a burning building; fit enough to respond to several emergencies in a day, sometimes without sleep; honest enough to be trusted inside every home and business in town; and compassionate and polite enough to interact with the public daily.

In most large cities, many more people apply for firefighting positions than can ever be accepted. A large percentage of people who apply fail one or more parts of the selection process: the written exam, the physical ability test, the oral interview or board, or one of the other steps in the process. You don't want to be one of those people.

That's one advantage you have over the competition: you're reading this book to get the inside scoop on the whole application process! This book will tell you what to expect every step of the way, so you'll know exactly what the steps are in becoming a firefighter. Knowing those steps, you'll have an edge over applicants coming in cold.

MUNICIPAL FIREFIGHTER SELECTION PROCESS

Since most career firefighters are employed as municipal firefighters (nine out of 10), their selection process deserves the most discussion. Also, many other fire departments (including private companies and military bases) have selection procedures that are similar to those for municipal firefighters.

The application process can be long and arduous because there are so many steps in it. The process goes far beyond merely filling out the application forms, although application forms can be long and unwieldy themselves. But don't fear, because this section will lead you through the entire application process, giving you tips and techniques for doing your very best and for increasing your chances of getting hired at the end of the process. You can find out how to make the most of each step of the application process before you begin by reading this section, and that way, you can stay a step ahead of the competition.

See the checklists below to get an overview of the process for landing the job you want. The first checklist outlines steps that you can take to land a career firefighting job and the second checklist contains additional requirements that some fire departments need you to follow.

Steps for Landing a Job

___ Read this book thoroughly

___ Graduate from high school or obtain a GED

___ Begin a physical conditioning work-out schedule

___ Enroll in a training program if you reside in a state that requires certification before you can become a firefighter (see chapter three for a list of programs near you)

___ Search for firefighter exam or position announcements

___ Request application forms from the fire departments you'd like to work for

___ Get your name on waiting lists to obtain applications from any departments who are not currently giving out applications

___ Carefully complete and submit all applications on or before their due dates

___ Prepare and study for the written exam by getting an exam preparation guide (see Appendix B for book titles)

___ Study this chapter very closely to find out what to expect on the physical and written exam and the oral interview

___ Take and pass the physical ability exam

___ Take and pass the written exam

___ Do well in the oral interview or board

___ Get state and/or county certification if necessary

___ Obtain additional training as an emergency medical technician (EMT) or as a paramedic to increase your chances for getting hired

___ Enroll in a fire science training program to enhance your marketability

___ Become a volunteer firefighter to gain experience and learn more about the field

___ Look on the Internet for job openings and job-related information

Additional Steps that May be Required

Here are several additional steps that are required in various states and municipalities, depending on their specific requirements. While not all fire departments require all of these steps, most departments require at least some of them, so be forearmed with the knowledge that you might need to do the following steps in addition to those listed above. You can call the departments you're interested in and ask them what their exact requirements include. You can also look up the specific requirements for several locations in one of the books mentioned in Appendix B under the heading *Preparing for Firefighter Exams.*

Additional Possible Requirements

___ Pass a drug screening test

___ Pass a psychological examination

___ Pass a medical examination

___ Pass a background investigation (may include checking your personal references, your criminal and driving record, and your fingerprints)

___ Provide proof of residency

___ Provide voter registration certificate

___ Provide proof of citizenship, such as birth certificate, naturalization papers, or baptismal papers

___ Possess a valid driver's license

___ Have uncorrected vision of at least 20/50 in both eyes; some fire departments require 20/20; others have no uncorrected limits

___ Pass a polygraph (lie detector) test that asks questions about your background and past drug use

___ Certify that you have not smoked a cigarette, cigar, or pipe in the past year

Getting the Exam or Position Announcement

Applying to be a firefighter differs from applying for most other jobs. The differences begin with the exam or position announcement. You rarely see fire department openings advertised in the Help Wanted section of the newspaper, as many other jobs are. Instead, the city usually starts looking for potential firefighters by means of a special announcement. This announcement will outline the basic qualifications for the position as well as the steps you will have to go through in the selection process. It often tells you some of the duties you will be expected to perform. It may give the date and place of the written exam, which is usually the first step in the selection process.

Get a copy of this announcement. Your public library may have a copy. Or you can get one directly from the fire department or city personnel department. If exams are held irregularly, the fire or personnel department may maintain a mailing list, so that you can receive an exam announcement the next time an exam is scheduled. If exams are held frequently, you will sometimes be told to simply show up at the exam site on a given day of the week or month. In those cases you usually get more information about the job and the selection process if you pass the written exam. Study the exam announcement, as well as any other material (such as brochures) that the department sends you.

What is an Eligibility List?

Most fire departments, or the city personnel departments that handle the selection process for them, establish a list of eligible candidates; many such lists rank candidates from highest to lowest. This list of applicants is commonly referred to as the *eligibility list*. How ranks are determined varies from place to place; sometimes the rank is based solely on the written exam score, sometimes on the physical ability test, and sometimes on a combination of factors. The point is, even if you make it through the entire selection process, the likelihood that you will be hired as a firefighter often depends on the quality of your performance in one or more parts of the selection process.

Make a commitment now: you need to work hard, in advance, to do well on the written exam, the physical ability test, and the oral interview (if there is one), so that your name will stand out at the top of your agency's eligibility list. You should aim to get 100 percent correct on every test to get a chance at coming out toward the top of the list. Some applicants may be getting extra points for living in the jurisdiction or for active military duty, so you need to score very high to compete with them. Often, firefighters on waiting lists will have scores of 100-105 due to extra points, so don't plan on merely passing with a score in the 70's or 80's if you want to get called from the eligibility list.

Filling Out the Application

Often the first step in the process of becoming a firefighter is filling out an application. Sometimes this is a real application, asking about your education, employment experience, personal data, and so on. Sometimes there's just an application to take the written or physical test, with a more complete application coming later. In any case, at some point

Application Tips

- If you have access to a typewriter, use it. If not, write as legibly as you can.

- Neatness and accuracy count. Filling in your apartment number in the blank labeled "city" reflects poorly on your ability to follow directions.

- Verify all information you put on the form—don't guess or estimate. If you're not sure of, for instance, the exact address of your high school or of what year you worked for a certain company, look it up.

- If you're mailing your application, take care to submit it to the proper address. It might go to the personnel department rather than to the fire department. Follow the directions on the exam announcement.

- Make a copy of your application before sending it in, so you can use it as a guide when filling out additional applications.

you will probably be asked some questions you wouldn't expect to see on a regular job application. You might be asked things like whether you've ever gotten any speeding tickets or been in trouble with the law, whether you've used illegal drugs, even whether any relatives work for the city or for the fire department. Your answers to these, as well as the more conventional questions, will serve as the starting point if the department conducts an investigation of your background, so it's important to answer all questions accurately and honestly.

Sample Applications

See the sample applications on the following pages to get an idea of what you might be filling out as an initial step in becoming a firefighter. These applications are provided as samples only, and they cannot be used to submit to any fire departments. You need to get an original application form from the appropriate department when you're ready to apply. However, you can read through these samples to find out what sort of information you'll be asked to provide—and to practice filling out the application. Don't underestimate this step. Filling out the application neatly and accurately can make or break your quest for employment because its a key part of the employment process.

City of Sacramento
Employment Application
Department of Human Resources
921 10th Street, Room 101, Sacramento, CA 95814
Telephone: (916) 264-5726 / TDD: (916) 264-7388
An Equal Opportunity/Affirmative Action Employer

INSTRUCTIONS: *This application is part of the examination process. It must be* <u>completely filled out</u> *and signed to be accepted for review. Late and/or incomplete applications will be rejected.*

PLEASE PRINT OR TYPE
SOCIAL SECURITY NUMBER _____ - _____ - _____

JOB/EXAMINATION TITLE: _____

NAME _____
　　　　Last　　　　　　　　　First　　　　　　Middle Initial

MAILING ADDRESS: _____
　　　　　　　Street #　　　Street Name　　　Apartment #

_____
　City　　　　　　　　　State　　　　　　Zip Code

Dept. of Human Resources Use Only	
App. Accepted	☐
App. Rejected	☐
Education	☐
Experience	☐
NMQ	☐
Late	☐
Other	☐

HOME PHONE ( )　_____　OTHER PHONE ( )　_____
ALL APPLICANTS, INCLUDING CITY EMPLOYEES, MUST IMMEDIATELY NOTIFY PERSONNEL SERVICES' STAFF, ROOM 200 AT THE ABOVE ADDRESS OF ANY ADDRESS OR PHONE CHANGES.

AGE: If applying for a sworn position in law enforcement or the fire service, will you be 21 or older at the application deadline date? _____YES _____NO

CALIFORNIA DRIVER LICENSE: If required for position, do you have one? ☐ Yes ☐ No
Dr. License # _____ Class _____ Expires _____

VETERAN'S PREFERENCE: Are you requesting Veteran's Preference? ☐ Yes ☐ No
To qualify for Veteran's Preference, a copy of Form DD214 must be submitted with this application. There are several criteria you must meet before qualifying for this preference. Please ask for the <u>VETERAN'S PREFERENCE REGULATIONS</u> sheet.

Active Duty - From _____ to _____

CONVICTIONS: Conviction of a crime is not necessarily a bar to employment. Each case is considered separately based on job requirements. However, failure to list convictions, except as provided below, may result in termination from the examination process or employment.
1. Have you ever been convicted by a court of a crime? ☐ Yes ☐ No
　Omit: a) Traffic violations (Driving Under the Influence Convictions must be reported).
　Omit: b) Any conviction committed prior to your 18th birthday which was finally adjudicated in Juvenile Court or under a youth offender law.
　Omit: c) Any incident sealed under Welfare and Institutions Code S781 or Penal Code S1203.45.

2. If "YES" state WHAT conviction, WHEN, WHERE, AND DISPOSITION OF CASE. _____

CITY EMPLOYMENT:
1. Are you currently employed by the City of Sacramento? ☐ Yes ☐ No
　If "YES", what department? _____
2. If "NO", have you ever been employed by the City of Sacramento? ☐ Yes ☐ No
　If "YES", what department? _____
　If you were previously employed by the City of Sacramento
　under another name, please state other name(s). _____
3. Please check the type(s) of work you will accept:
　☐ Permanent employment　☐ Full-time　☐ Part-time　☐ Temporary (12 months maximum in any one job).

EDUCATION AND TRAINING:
Complete this section if required for job. Submit verification of your education such as <u>copies</u> of transcripts or diplomas.
High School Graduate or Passed GED? ☐ Yes ☐ No

NAME AND LOCATION OF COLLEGE, UNIVERSITY, BUSINESS, CORRESPONDENCE, TRADE OR SERVICE SCHOOL(S)	MAJOR COURSE OF STUDY	Completed # of		Diploma, Certificate, or Degree Received, # Hours of Training Program, or Course(s) Required by Job Announcement
		Semester Units	Quarter Units	

Current certificates of professional competence, licenses, membership in professional associations. _____

EMPLOYMENT QUESTIONNAIRE

APPLICANT: Please complete both sides of this section and submit it with your application. This completed section is confidential and will be detached from your application. This information is voluntary and is gathered in accordance with State and Federal laws for the purpose of evaluating the effectiveness of our Affirmative Action and recruitment efforts.

CHECK MALE OR FEMALE. ☐ Male ☐ Female
ALSO, PLEASE CHECK ONE BOX ONLY FOR THE RACIAL/ETHNIC CATEGORY YOU MOST CLOSELY IDENTIFY WITH.
(SEE BELOW FOR THE ETHNIC DEFINITIONS.)

☐ White　(Not Hispanic origin) All persons having origins in any of the original peoples of Europe, North Africa, or the Middle East.
☐ Black　(Not of Hispanic origin) All persons having origins in any of the Black racial groups of Africa.
☐ Hispanic　All persons of Mexican, Puerto Rican, Cuban, any other Spanish Hispanic (does not include persons of Portuguese or Brazilian origin or persons who acquire Spanish surname).
☐ Asian or　All persons having origins in any of the original peoples of the Far East, Southeast Asia, the Indian Subcontinent, or the Pacific Islands (excluding the Philippine
　Pacific Islander　Islands). This area includes, for example, China, Japan, Korea, and Samoa.
☐ American Indian　All persons having origins in any of the original peoples of North America, and who maintain cultural identifications through tribal affiliation or community recognition.
　or Alaskan Native　Please identify your tribal affiliation: _____

JOB/EXAMINATION TITLE: _____ NAME_____

Last   First   Middle Initial

QUALIFYING EXPERIENCE: *List experience which relates to the qualifications required on the Job Announcement. Begin with your most recent experience. List all jobs separately. The experience you list will be used to determine if you meet the qualifications stated on the job announcement. Applications that do not list related experience will be considered incomplete and will be rejected. A resume will not substitute for the information required in this section. Your application will be rejected if you write "See Resume".*

NOTE: If you have additional experience and/or comments, please attached another sheet. Qualifying experience is based on 40 hours per week (pro-rated if less than 40 hours/week).

FROM: MO. DAY YR.	TITLE:	PRESENT OR MOST RECENT EMPLOYER:
TO: MO. DAY YR.	DUTIES:	
Total time: YR. MO.		ADDRESS:
HOURS per WEEK:		
# PEOPLE SUPERVISED:		PHONE:
MONTHLY SALARY:		SUPERVISOR:
		May we contact? ☐ YES ☐ NO
FROM: MO. DAY YR.	TITLE:	FORMER EMPLOYER:
TO: MO. DAY YR.	DUTIES:	
Total Time: YR. MO.		ADDRESS:
HOURS per WEEK:		
# PEOPLE SUPERVISED:		PHONE:
MONTHLY SALARY:		SUPERVISOR:
		May we contact? ☐ YES ☐ NO
FROM: MO. DAY YR.	TITLE:	FORMER EMPLOYER:
TO: MO. DAY YR.	DUTIES:	
Total Time: YR. MO.		ADDRESS:
HOURS per WEEK:		
# PEOPLE SUPERVISED:		PHONE:
MONTHLY SALARY:		SUPERVISOR:
		May we contact? ☐ YES ☐ NO
FROM: MO. DAY YR.	TITLE:	FORMER EMPLOYER:
TO: MO. DAY YR.	DUTIES:	
Total Time: YR. MO.		ADDRESS:
HOURS per WEEK:		
# PEOPLE SUPERVISED:		PHONE:
MONTHLY SALARY:		SUPERVISOR:
		May we contact? ☐ YES ☐ NO

I CERTIFY that all statements in this application are true and complete. I agree and understand that any misstatements or omissions of material facts herein will cause forfeiture on my part of all rights to employment with the City of Sacramento. I understand that if i do not meet the announced requirements, I will be eliminated from the examination process, and that applications must be received by the City Department of Human Resources at 921 10th Street, Room 101, Sacramento CA 95814, by 5:00 p.m. on the final filing date specified on the Job Announcement. **POSTMARKS ARE NOT ACCEPTED.** I herby authorize the city to verify the accuracy of the information I have provided on this application.

SIGNATURE: _____   DATE:_____

(Required for application to be complete)

THIS APPLICATION AND ALL ATTACHMENTS ARE CONSIDERED PROPERTY OF THE CITY OF SACRAMENTO DEPARTMENT OF HUMAN RESOURCES. PHOTOCOPIES WILL <u>NOT</u> BE FURNISHED. PLEASE ATTACH <u>COPIES</u> OF YOUR ORIGINAL DOCUMENTS.

Job/Examination Title: _____

I first learned of this job opening through (check one only):

☐ A Friend or Relative
☐ The City's Department of Human Resources Job Line or Walk In
☐ Contact with a City Department/Employee
      If Department, Specify Which
☐ An Organization or Group (Specify) _____
☐ An Advertisement (Specify Newspaper, Publication,
      TV or Radio Station) _____
☐ Other Means (Specify) _____

Do you have any physical or mental impairment which may limit your ability to perform the job applied for?   ☐ YES   ☐ NO
If yes, what can be done to accommodate your limitations and, if necessary, to provide assistance in the testing process?

_____

_____

Revised January 25, 1996/FRM2-16.C

PER 029

CITY OF HOUSTON
PERSONNEL DEPARTMENT
P.O. BOX 1562
HOUSTON, TEXAS 77251

An Equal Opportunity Employer

EMPLOYMENT
APPLICATION

Please Print In Ink Or Type

Position:	PN#	Today's Date

PERSONAL

Last Name	First	Middle	Social Security # Must be verified

No.	Street	City	State	Zip	Home Phone	Business/Alternate Phone

U. S. Citizenship	If not a citizen, do you possess a work authorization?
YES ☐ NO ☐	Number and Type

If you have ever been convicted of an offense (excluding minor traffic violations) complete the following:

Charge	Place of Arrest	Date	What Disposition was Made?

Please list below any relatives, including those by marriage, employed by the City:

Name of Relative	Relationship	Department	Position

Have you ever been employed by the City of Houston? ☐ YES NO ☐	Position Held	Date of Separation
Under what name did you appear on payroll?		

Do Not Write In This Space

EDUCATION

	Name & Location	Date Graduated		Degree	If no, highest yr or hrs compl.	Major
		YES	NO			
High School						
College or University						
Graduate School						
Trade/Business/Technical						
Armed Service School						

MILITARY

Branch of Service	Service Dates		Rank at Discharge	Are you now a member of any military or naval organization?
	From	To		YES ☐ NO ☐

Do you have a valid Texas driver's license? ☐ YES NO ☐

(TEXAS DRIVER'S LICENSE NUMBER)
(Class A, P, or C)

PER 029 REV. 2/93

List below beginning with your most recent, all present and past employment.
Please complete in full.

	Name & Address of Company	Position, Dates Emp. & Salary		Supv. Name & Title	Reason for Leaving
1		From Mo/Yr	Current $	Name	
				Title	
		To Mo/Yr	Final $		
2		From Mo/Yr		Name	
				Title	
		To Mo/Yr	Final $		
3		From Mo/Yr		Name	
				Title	
		To Mo/Yr	Final $		
4		From Mo/Yr		Name	
				Title	
		To Mo/Yr	Final $		
5		From Mo/Yr		Name	
				Title	
		To Mo/Yr	Final $		

(Left margin vertical label: EMPLOYMENT HISTORY)

List below three references (other than relatives)

Name	Phone	Address	Employer

(Left margin vertical label: REFERENCES)

MAY WE CONTACT YOUR PRESENT EMPLOYER FOR REFERENCE? _____

PLEASE READ CAREFULLY BEFORE SIGNING: I certify that all the information provided by me in connection with my application, whether on this document or not, is true and complete, and I understand that any misstatement, falsification, or omission of information shall be grounds for refusal to hire or, if hired, termination. I authorize any of the persons, organizations, and educational institutions referenced in this application to give officials of the City of Houston any and all information concerning my previous employment, education, or any other information they might have, personal or otherwise, with regard to any of the subjects covered by this application, and I release all such parties from all liability from any damages which may result from furnishing such information to the City of Houston.

I UNDERSTAND THAT ALL PERSONS OFFERED EMPLOYMENT BY THE CITY OF HOUSTON MUST SUCCESS-FULLY PASS A DRUG TEST AS A CONDITION OF EMPLOYMENT.

Signature of Applicant _____

Date _____

Taking the Written Exam

In most jurisdictions, taking a written exam is the next step in the application process, though in some cases the physical ability test comes first. The written exam is your first opportunity to show that you have what it takes to become a firefighter. As such, it's extremely important. People who don't pass the written exam don't go any farther in the selection process. Furthermore, the written exam score often figures into applicants' rank on the eligibility list; in some cases, this score by itself determines your rank, while in others it is combined with other scores, such as physical ability or oral board scores. The exam bulletin may specify what your rank will be based on.

Written exams for most municipal fire departments test basic skills and aptitudes: how well you understand what you read, your ability to follow directions, your judgment and reasoning skills, your ability to read and understand maps and floor plans, and sometimes your memory or your math. In this type of preliminary written exam, *you will not be tested on your knowledge of fire behavior, firefighting procedures, or any other specific body of knowledge.* This test is designed only to see if you can read, reason, and do basic math. In some places, taking the exam involves studying written materials in advance and then answering questions about them on the exam. These written materials generally have to do with fire and firefighting—but all you have to do is study the guide you're given. You're still being tested just on your reading skills and memory, and there are good reasons for this.

Firefighters have to be able to read, understand, and act on complex written materials—not only fire law and fire procedures, but also scientific materials about fire, combustible materials, chemicals, and so forth. An experienced firefighter from Dallas, Texas says:

> Some people think that all you need is physical strength and a hefty dose of courage to become a good firefighter. That is a typical misconception that the public often has about what it takes to become a firefighter. In reality, we have to know a lot about fire and smoke and how they are affected by a building's construction. We have to know how fire travels, what will make it larger, what part of buildings are the most dangerous, and a lot of other scientific things. In order to gain the necessary knowledge, we undergo training programs on a regular basis. If you don't have basic math, reading, and reasoning skills, you won't be able to cut it as a firefighter.

Indeed, firefighters have to be able to think clearly and independently, because lives depend on decisions they make in a split second. They have to be able to do enough math to read and understand pressure gauges or estimate the height of a building and the amount of hose needed to reach to the third floor. They have to be able to read maps so they can get to the emergency site quickly, and floor plans so that they can find their way to an exit—even in a smoke-filled building.

Most exams are multiple-choice tests of the sort you've often encountered in school. You get an exam book and an answer sheet where you have to fill in little circles (bubbles) or squares with a number-two pencil.

Written Exam Tips

- Ask for and *use* any material the fire department or personnel department publishes about the written test. Some agencies have study guides; some even conduct study sessions. Why let others get a vital advantage while you don't?

- Locate and read test preparation books that are geared for firefighting written exams to increase your score. See Appendix B for a list of useful test preparation books.

- Practice, practice, practice by taking several practice tests. And then practice some more.

- Try to find people who have taken the exam recently, and ask them about what was on the exam. Their hindsight—"I wish I had. . ."—can be your foresight.

Applicants are generally notified in writing about their performance on the exam. The notification may simply say whether or not you passed, or it may tell you what your score was. It may also say when you should show up for the next step in the process, which is often the physical ability test.

Taking the Physical Ability Test

The physical ability test is the next step in the process for many fire departments; however, some put this step first. You may have to bring a note from your doctor saying that you are in good enough shape to undertake this test before you will be allowed to participate. The fire department wants to make sure that no one has a heart attack in the middle of the test. This is a clue: expect the test to be tough.

Firefighting is, after all, physically demanding work. Once again, lives depend on whether your strength, stamina, and overall fitness allow you to carry out the necessary tasks during an emergency. If you make it to the academy and later into a fire company, you can expect to continue physical training and exercises throughout your career. In fact, in some cities all firefighters are required to retake the physical ability test every year.

The exact events that make up the physical ability test vary from place to place, but the tasks you have to perform are almost always job-related—they're a lot like the physical tasks you will actually have to perform as a firefighter. Many times the test is set up like an obstacle course, and usually the test is timed, with a cutoff time for passing. Often you have to wear full (heavy) protective gear, including an air pack, throughout these events. Here's an example of the events in a test that you would typically have five to seven minutes to complete:

- Dummy drag
- Hose drag
- Climb stairs
- Climb through tunnel
- Raise and climb ladder
- Jump over wall

In an obstacle-course setup like this one, you might be given the opportunity to walk the course before you actually have to take the test. If you have the chance, definitely take a walk-through first. In departments where the physical ability test figures into your rank on the eligibility list, merely meeting the maximum time to pass isn't good enough; people who have faster times will be higher on the list than you are. You can usually find out just what tasks are included in the physical ability test from the exam announcement or related materials.

Different departments have different policies on retesting if you fail. Some allow you to retest on the same day after a rest period. Some allow you to come back another time and try again, usually up to a set maximum number of tries. And in some departments, your first try is the only chance you get; if you fail, you're out, at least until the next testing period. Not many departments will allow you to retest, if you have already passed, simply to better your time. A prospective firefighter from Palm Harbor, Florida has this to say about the physical ability tests:

> All physical ability tests are different, depending on the fire department's equipment and course set-up. I've taken physical ability tests for five different municipal fire departments in the last year and a half and some were much harder than others. Don't be fooled into thinking all physical tests are easy if you happen to take one that doesn't seem very difficult. The next one might be a killer. I'm in great shape, but I just took a test that was a lot harder than the four

I'd taken previously. My advice is to do a lot of running to prepare for physical ability tests because the tough tests really take a lot of endurance.

Many urban fire departments report that the physical ability test is the one step of the process in which the most applicants fail. People come in unprepared, they're simply not strong enough or fast enough to do all the events, while wearing heavy gear, in the time allotted. Female applicants, in particular, have high failure rates on physical ability tests because some of the events require a lot of upper-body strength.

But don't despair. The physical ability test is one area where advance preparation is almost guaranteed to pay off. No matter how good of shape you're in, start an exercise program *now*. You can design your program around the requirements listed in the exam announcement if you want, but any exercise that will increase your strength and stamina will help. Because sheer brute force is required to drag a 150-pound dummy or to lift a 50-foot ladder, exercises that increase your strength are particularly important. But you'll also want to include some aerobic exercise such as running or swimming to improve your stamina and overall fitness as well.

If you're *not* in great shape, consult a doctor before you begin an exercise program. Start slow and easy and increase your activity as you go. As you gain strength, start wearing weights on your ankles and wrists, and later add a backpack stuffed with dictionaries or rocks. And remember that you don't have to do all this work alone. Working out with someone else not only is more fun, but it also helps guard against the temptation to cheat by skipping a day or doing fewer "reps."

Physical Ability Exam Tips

- Take advantage of any training sessions or test-course walk-throughs the fire department offers. The whole purpose of such sessions is to help you pass the physical test.

- Start exercising *now*. Yes, today. Work up to a 45-minute workout at least five times a week.

- Exercises that increase your upper-body strength are particularly useful. Consider lifting weights several times a week.

- If you smoke, stop.

- If you're overweight, diet along with your exercise.

- Exercise with a friend. Listen to tunes while you work out. Give yourself rewards for reaching milestones like shaving a minute off your mile-run time or bench-pressing ten more pounds.

The Background Investigation

Most fire departments conduct background investigations of applicants who pass the written and physical tests. Firefighters have to be honest, upright citizens who can get along with both their company and the people they serve, so the fire department conducts a background investigation to make sure you're the right kind of person. You may not even know such an investigation is going on—until someone at the oral interview asks you why you wrote on your application that you never used drugs when your high school friends all say you regularly smoked marijuana on weekends. (That's why it's important to answer honestly on your application.)

Some departments will investigate you in great depth, asking their contacts how long and how well they knew you and what kind of person they found you to be. Did you meet your obligations? How did you deal with problems? Did they find you to be an honest person? Do they know of anything that might affect your fitness to be a firefighter? The references you provided will lead the investigator to other people who knew you, and when the investigator is finished, he or she will have a pretty complete picture of what kind of person you are.

Other fire departments conduct a fairly superficial check, calling your former employers and schools simply to verify that you were there when you say you were there and didn't cause any problems during that time.

A few fire departments include a polygraph, or "lie detector" test as part of the background investigation. As long as you've been honest in what you've said when your stress reactions weren't being monitored by a polygraph machine, a lie detector test is nothing to worry about.

The best way you can improve your chances of getting through a background investigation with flying colors is by working on any problems in your background. You can't change the past, exactly, but you can use the present to improve your chances in the future. You can address problems that might give a background investigator pause: pay your old traffic tickets, get that juvenile offense that the lawyer said wouldn't "count" officially expunged from your record, document your full recovery from a serious illness or your drug-free status since high school.

The Oral Interview

The selection process in most fire departments includes one or more oral interviews. In some cities, applicants who get this far in the process meet with the fire chief or deputy fire chief, who may conduct something like a typical job interview. The chief or deputy chief might describe in detail what the job is like, ask you how well you think you can do a job like that, and ask you why you want to be a firefighter in the first place. In the process, the chief will also be assessing your interpersonal skills, whether you seem honest and (relatively) comfortable in talking to him or her. You may also be asked questions about your background and experience.

This interview can be a make-or-break part of the process, with the chief turning thumbs up or down to your candidacy, or the chief may rank you against other applicants, in which case the chief's assessment of you is likely to figure into your place on the eligibility list.

The chief's interview may also include situational questions like those typically asked by an oral board. When you're asked a situational question, you are given a sample situation that is common in fighting fires and then asked what you would do in that situation. You may be facing an oral board in addition to or in place of your interview with the chief.

The Oral Board

An oral board is similar to a job interview with a fire chief, only in an oral board, there are several members who sit on a panel and ask you questions. The oral board typically assesses such qualities as interpersonal skills, communication skills, judgment and decision-making abilities, respect for diversity, and adaptability. The board itself consists of two to five people, who may be a combination of firefighters and civilian personnel or interview specialists. There's usually some variety in the makeup of the board: officers of various ranks and/or civilians from the personnel department or from the community.

The way the interview is conducted depends on the practices of the individual department. You may be asked a few questions similar to those you would be asked at a normal employment interview: "Why do you want to be a firefighter?" "What qualities do you have that would make you good at this job?" You may be asked questions about your background, especially if your application or background investigation raised any questions in the board members' minds. Have answers prepared for any questions you can think of that would be asked about your background, in case they come up during the board interview.

Instead of or in addition to such questions, you may be presented with hypothetical situations that you will be asked to respond to. A board member may say something like this: "After a dwelling fire is under control, you're walking through the building checking its structural soundness. When you walk into the living room, you see a fellow firefighter sticking a gold watch into the pocket of his coat. What would you do?" You would then have to come up with an appropriate response to this situation.

Increasingly, cities have standardized the oral board questions. The same questions are asked of every candidate, and when the interview is over the board rates each candidate on a standard scale. This procedure helps the interviewers reach a somewhat more objective conclusion about the candidates they have interviewed and may result in a score that is included in the factors used to rank candidates in the eligibility list.

A career firefighter from California has this advice to give prospective firefighters who complete an oral interview or an oral board:

> As soon as you leave, take out a pen and paper and write down as many of the questions that you can remember that were asked during the session. Then, think about your responses to the questions and how you could make them better. Take time to synthesize your responses to those questions and come up with additional ways you can respond in the future. Chances are that you'll be asked similar questions in another interview. This way you can prepare ahead of time for the next interview or oral board that you'll face.

How to Prepare for the Oral Board or Interview

If the fire department you're applying to hands out any material about the oral board, study it carefully. It may tell you what the board is looking for. It may even give you some sample questions you can practice with.

Whether you're facing an oral board or an individual interview, think about your answers to questions you might be asked. You might even try to write your own oral board questions and situations. Write down your answers if you want. Practice saying them in front of a mirror until you feel comfortable, but don't memorize them. You don't want to sound like you're reciting from a book. Your answers should sound conversational even though you've prepared in advance.

Then enlist friends or family to serve as a mock oral board or interviewer. If you know a speech teacher, get him or her to help. Give them your questions, tell them about what you've learned, and then have a practice oral board or interview. Start from the moment you walk into the room. Go through the entire session as if it were the real thing, and then ask your mock board or interviewer for feedback

Oral Board or Interview Tips

- Dress neatly and conservatively, as you would for a business interview.

- Be polite; say "please" and "thank you," "sir" and "ma'am."

- Remember, one-half of communication is listening. Look at board members or interviewers as they speak to you, and listen carefully to what they say.

- Think before you speak. Nod or say "OK" to indicate that you understand the question, and then pause a moment to collect your thoughts before speaking.

- If you start to feel nervous, take a deep breath, relax, and count to five to regain composure.

on your performance. It may even help to videotape your mock board session. The camera can reveal things about your body language or habits that you don't even know about.

The Psychological Evaluation

Some cities, though not all, include a psychological evaluation as part of the firefighter selection process. The fire department wants to make sure that you are emotionally and mentally stable before putting you in a high-stress job in which you have to interact with peers, superiors, and the public. Don't worry, though; the psychological evaluation is not designed to uncover your deep dark secrets. Its only purpose is to make sure you have the mental and emotional health to do the job.

If your fire department has a psychological evaluation, most likely that means you'll be taking one or two written tests. A few cities have candidates interviewed by a psychologist or psychiatrist.

If you have to take a written psychological test, it is likely to be a standardized multiple-choice or true-false test licensed from a psychological testing company. The Minnesota Multiphasic Personality Inventory (MMPI) is one commonly used test. Such tests typically ask you about your interests, attitudes, and background. They may take one hour or several; the hiring agency will let you know approximately how much time to allot.

If you need to take an oral psychological assessment, you'll meet with a psychologist or psychiatrist, who may be either on the hiring agency's staff or an independent contractor. The psychologist may ask you questions about your schooling and jobs, your relationships with family and friends, your habits, or your hobbies. The psychologist may be as interested in the way you answer—whether you come across as open, forthright, and honest—as in the answers themselves.

Don't try to "psych-out" the assessment. The psychologists who designed the written test know more about psyching-out tests than you do. They designed the test so that one answer checks against another to find out whether test-takers are lying. Just answer openly and honestly, and don't worry about how your answers will sound to the psychologist.

The Medical Examination

Before passage of the Americans With Disabilities Act (ADA), many fire departments conducted a medical examination early in the selection process, before the physical ability test. Now, the ADA says it's illegal to do any medical examinations or ask any questions that could reveal an applicant's disability until after a conditional offer of employment has been made. That means that in most jurisdictions you will get such a conditional offer before you are asked to submit to a medical exam.

You should know, however, that almost any disability is grounds for disqualification as a firefighter, even under the protections provided by ADA. Firefighting requires a high level of physical and mental fitness, and a host of disabilities that would not prevent a candidate from doing some other job would prevent a firefighter from fulfilling essential job functions. Even, for instance, a skin condition that requires a man to wear facial hair would disqualify that man from being a firefighter, because facial hair interferes with proper operation of the breathing apparatus.

What the Medical Exam Is Like

The medical exam itself is nothing to be afraid of. It will be just like any other thorough physical exam. The doctor may be on the staff of the hiring agency or someone outside the department with his or her own practice, just like your own doctor. Your blood pressure, temperature, weight, and so on will be measured; your heart and lungs will be listened to and your limbs examined. The doctor will peer into your eyes, ears, nose, and mouth, and conduct a thorough medical exam. You'll also have to donate some blood and urine. Because of these tests, you won't know the results of the physical exam right away. You'll probably be notified in writing in a few weeks, after the test results come in.

Drug Testing

A test for use of illegal drugs *can* be administered before a conditional offer of employment. Because firefighters have to be in tip top physical shape, and because they are in a position of public trust, the fire department expects you to be drug-free. Indeed, you may have to undergo drug testing periodically throughout your career as a firefighter.

IF AT FIRST YOU DON'T SUCCEED, PART ONE

The selection process for firefighters is a rigorous one. If you fail one of the steps or do poorly on one of the exams, take time for some serious self-evaluation, so you can do better the next time around. Here are some tips on how you can evaluate your performance on the different steps of the application process.

The Written Test

If you didn't pass the written test, examine the reasons why you didn't do well. Was it just that the format was unfamiliar? Well, now you know what to expect. Do you need to brush up on some of the skills tested? There are lots of books out there to help people with basic skills. You might start with the LearningExpress *Skill Builder* books (See Appendix B for a list of helpful books). Enlist a teacher or a friend to help you, or check out the inexpensive courses offered by local high schools and community colleges. Some fire departments allow you to retest after a waiting period—a period you can use to improve your skills. If the exam isn't being offered again for years, consider trying a different jurisdiction.

The Physical Ability Test

If you don't pass the physical test, your course of action is clear. Increase your daily physical exercise until you *know* you can do what is required, and then retest or try another jurisdiction.

The Oral Board or Interview

If you don't pass the oral board or interview, try to figure out what the problem was. Do you think your answers were good but perhaps you didn't express them well? Then you need some practice in oral communication. You can take courses or enlist your friends to help you practice.

Did the questions and situations throw you for a loop, so you gave what now seem like inappropriate answers? Then spend time practicing answering similar questions for the next time. Talk to candidates who were successful and ask them what they said. Talk with firefighters you know about what might have been good answers for the questions you were asked. Even if your department doesn't allow you to redo the oral board, you can use what you learn when applying to another fire department.

The Medical Exam

If the medical exam eliminates you, you will usually be notified as to what condition caused the problem. Is the condition one that can be corrected? See your doctor for advice.

Other Reasons

If you don't make the eligibility list and aren't told why, the problem might have been the oral board or the psychological evaluation or the background investigation. Now you really have to do some hard thinking. Can you think of *anything* in your past that might lead to questions about your fitness to be a firefighter? Could any of your personal traits or attitudes raise such questions? And then the hard question: Is there anything you can do to change these aspects of your past or your personality? If so, you might have a chance when you reapply or apply to another department. If not, it's time to think about another field.

If you feel you were wrongly excluded on the basis of a psychological evaluation or background check, most departments have appeals procedures. However, that word *wrongly* is very important. The psychologist or background investigator almost certainly had to supply a rationale in recommending that the department not hire you. Do you have solid factual evidence that you can use in an administrative hearing to counter such a rationale? If not, you'd be wasting your time and money, as well as the hiring agency's, by making an appeal. Move carefully and get legal advice before you take such a step.

The Waiting Game

You went through the whole long process, passed all the tests, did the best you could, made the eligibility list—and now you wait. You *could* just sit on your hands. Or you could decide to *do* something with this time to prepare for what you hope is your new career. Do some networking. Talk to firefighters about what the job is really like. Find out if your fire department offers volunteer opportunities or a cadet program. Take a course in first aid or enroll in an Emergency Medical Technician program. Even if you don't get called, and even if your rank on the eligibility list doesn't get you a job this time, you'll be better qualified for the next try.

Here's one thing you *don't* want to do while you're waiting: Don't keep calling the fire department to find out what your chances are or how far down on the list they've gotten or when they might call you. You probably won't get to talk to the people making those decisions, so you'll just annoy some poor receptionist. If you did get through to the decision-makers, you'd be in even worse shape: you'd be annoying *them*.

IF AT FIRST YOU DON'T SUCCEED, PART TWO

If you make the eligibility list, go through the waiting game, and finally aren't selected, don't despair. Think through all the steps of the selection process again, and use them to do a critical self-evaluation. Maybe your written, physical, or oral board score was high enough to pass but not high enough to put you at the top of the list. At the next testing, make sure you're better prepared.

Maybe you had an excellent score that should have put you at the top of the list, and you suspect that you were passed over for someone lower down. That means someone less well qualified was selected while you were not, right? Maybe, maybe not. There were probably a lot of people on the list, and a lot of them may have scored high. One more point on the test might have made the difference, or maybe the department had the freedom to pick and choose on the basis of other qualifications. Maybe, in comparison with you, a lot of people on the eligibility list had more education or experience.

Perhaps there were plenty of certified Emergency Medical Technicians or Paramedics on the list, and they got first crack at the available jobs. And yes, members of minority groups and veterans may have been given preference in hiring. Whether or not you think that's fair, you can be assured that it was a conscious decision on the part of the hiring agency; it may even have been mandated from above.

What can you do? You've heard or read about law suits being brought against cities by people who thought their selection process was unfair. That's definitely a last resort, a step you would take only after getting excellent legal advice and thinking through the significant costs of time, money, and energy. You'd also have to think about whether you'd want to occupy a position you got as the result of a lawsuit and whether you'd be hurting your chances of being hired somewhere else. Most people are better off simply trying again.

It Takes Time

Don't get discouraged if you don't get hired by the first fire department you apply to. In fact, chances are that it will take several tries before you land your dream job. There's a lot of competition out there and not enough openings for everyone to land a job their first time around. Many firefighters have had to persevere for several years before landing a job. A firefighter in Colorado says:

> It took me a lot of time to get on—almost 5 years, and I had a lot of experience behind me. You need to continually update your education and work on your oral skills. I know people who tried for 8 years before they finally made it. It's all worth it in the end. My department just hired a 31-year-old man who has been trying to land a full-time paid position since he was 23, so you can see that it takes time. You have to be patient.

This firefighter's experience is by no means unique. Many firefighters who were recently hired say that it took them a long time to make it into the department they wanted. In fact, a firefighter in California says:

> I was recently hired as a Firefighter/Paramedic with the American Rural Fire Protection District in California. Getting this job was a dream come true. I have been testing for over four years, taking classes, and volunteering my time, but I feel that it has all been worth it. I love my job, and I plan to stay in this department until I retire.

IF YOU DO SUCCEED

Congratulations! The end of the waiting game for you is notification to attend the fire service academy. You're on the road to your career as a firefighter. The road is hardly over, though. First, you have to make it through the academy, where you can expect physical training as well as training in fire and emergency services. (See chapter five for more information.) You'll also have a lot of learning to do during your first year or so on the job. Throughout your career, you'll need to keep up with new techniques, new equipment, and new procedures. And if you decide to go for a promotion, there will be more steps, more tests, more evaluations. But you can do it, if you're determined and committed. You've already made a good start.

STATE OR FEDERAL WILDAND FIREFIGHTER SELECTION PROCESS

The selection process to find new firefighters for state and federal government agencies is usually shorter and less involved than that of the municipal selection process. Another difference is that the selection process is on a much larger scale since state and federal agencies normally need to hire a much larger group of firefighters than each local government agency does. Also, most wildland firefighter positions are seasonal, so there tends to be significant turnover in the ranks.

While each state and federal agency has their own selection process, there are some things they have in common. You normally have to pass a physical ability test. For example, a state agency located in Idaho requires candidates to take two physical tests: one test requires applicants to run one and a half miles in 11 minutes and the second test requires applicants to run for three miles with a 45 pound pack on their back within 45 minutes. Many state and federal agencies also require that a short firefighter training course be completed. These training courses may last anywhere from a few hours to a few days to a week or more.

After being hired, wildland firefighter applicants normally need to pass a one-week training course in fighting wildland fires. Applicants who have not yet been hired can also take the training course, but they need to sign a waiver relieving the training company of responsibility if they have any physical problems during the training course. Most week-long training courses offer students what is commonly referred to as a *pink card* or *red card*—a small card that wildland firefighters carry with them that specifies their firefighting qualifications.

How to Apply

Contact the state or federal agencies that are located near the area in which you want to work to request an application. A good place to start is by calling the state or federal forests in the state in which you want to work. You can look in the phone book, check with your local public library, or find information on the Internet to find contact information for state and federal agencies that hire firefighters in specific locations. See Appendix A for national addresses of federal agencies that hire firefighters. You can also access some agencies' information on-line—refer to the section entitled *Using the Internet to Help Land the Job You Want* found later in this chapter for more information.

To apply for federal government positions, you may use the Application for Federal Employment, the Optional Application for Federal Employment (OF612), or a resume that includes all of the information requested by the publication entitled *Applying for a Federal Job* (OF512). You can call the Career America Connection to find information about available federal jobs at 912-757-3000 or 206-553-0888. The best times to apply are during the months of February and May, although you can call for information at any time during the year.

Sample Application

See the sample application on the following pages to get an idea of what you might be filling out as an initial step in becoming a federal firefighter. This application is provided as a sample only and cannot be used to submit for a job. You need to get an original application form from the appropriate department when you're ready to apply. However, you can read through the sample to find out what sort of information you'll be asked to provide—and to practice filling out the application. Don't underestimate this step. Filling out the application neatly and accurately can make or break your quest for employment because it's a key part of the employment process.

Form Approved
OMB No. 3206-0219

OPTIONAL APPLICATION FOR FEDERAL EMPLOYMENT - OF 612

You may apply for most jobs with a resume, this form, or other written format. If your resume or application does not provide all the information requested on this form and in the job vacancy announcement, you may lose consideration for a job.

1 Job title in announcement	2 Grade(s) applying for	3 Announcement number

4 Last name	First and middle names	5 Social Security Number

6 Mailing address	7 Phone numbers (include area code) Daytime ( )
City State ZIP Code	Evening ( )

WORK EXPERIENCE

8 Describe your paid and nonpaid work experience related to the job for which you are applying. Do not attach job descriptions.

1) Job title (if Federal, include series and grade)

From (MM/YY)	To (MM/YY)	Salary $	per	Hours per week

Employer's name and address	Supervisor's name and phone number ( )

Describe your duties and accomplishments

2) Job title (if Federal, include series and grade)

From (MM/YY)	To (MM/YY)	Salary $	per	Hours per week

Employer's name and address	Supervisor's name and phone number ( )

Describe your duties and accomplishments

50612-101   NSN 7540-01-351-9178   Optional Form 612 (September 1994)
U.S. Office of Personnel Management

SAMPLE

9 May we contact your current supervisor?

        YES [   ]   **NO [   ]**► If we need to contact your current supervisor before making an offer, we will contact you first.

EDUCATION

10 Mark highest level completed. **Some HS [ ]**   **HS/GED [ ]**   **Associate [ ]**   **Bachelor [ ]**   **Master [ ]**   **Doctoral [ ]**

11 Last high school (HS) or GED school. Give the school's name, city, State, ZIP Code (if known), and year diploma or GED received.

12 Colleges and universities attended. Do **not** attach a copy of your transcript unless requested.

	Name		Total Credits Earned		Major(s)	Degree - Year
			Semester	Quarter		(if any) Received
1)	City	State ZIP Code				
2)						
3)						

OTHER QUALIFICATIONS

13 **Job-related** training courses (give title and year). **Job-related** skills (other languages, computer software/hardware, tools, machinery, typing speed, etc.). **Job-related** certificates and licenses (current only). **Job-related** honors, awards, and special accomplishments (publications, memberships in professional/honor societies, leadership activities, public speaking, and performance awards). Give dates, but do **not** send documents unless requested.

GENERAL

14 Are you a U.S. citizen?   **YES [ ]**   **NO [ ]**► Give the country of your citizenship. _____

15 Do you claim veterans' preference? **NO [ ]**   **YES [ ]**► Mark your claim of 5 or 10 points below.
    5 points [ ]► Attach your DD 214 or other proof. **10 points [ ]**► Attach an *Application for 10-Point Veterans' Preference* (SF 15) and proof required.

16 Were you ever a Federal civilian employee?   **NO [ ]**   **YES [ ]**► For highest civilian grade give: Series   Grade From (MM/YY) To (MM/YY)

17 Are you eligible for reinstatement based on career or career-conditional Federal status?
    NO [ ]   **YES [ ]**► If requested, attach SF 50 proof.

APPLICANT CERTIFICATION

18 **I certify** that, to the best of my knowledge and belief, all of the information on and attached to this application is true, correct, complete and made in good faith. **I understand** that false or fraudulent information on or attached to this application may be grounds for not hiring me or for firing me after I begin work, and may be punishable by fine or imprisonment. **I understand** that any information I give may be investigated.

SIGNATURE   **DATE SIGNED**

MILITARY FIREFIGHTER SELECTION PROCESS

If you would like to go the military route to becoming a firefighter, you need to join the military as the first step of the selection process. You'll need to meet the basic requirements for entering the military (see chapter one for a list of minimum requirements). The next step is to talk to military recruiters to find out how you can get a guarantee of being trained and placed in the fire protection field within the military. You must meet a number of specific requirements in order to qualify for a guaranteed firefighter career area; check with your local recruiting agent to find out exactly what steps you need to take.

The Armed Services Vocational Aptitude Battery (ASVAB)

Many high schools and post-secondary schools offer the ASVAB test to students. It is also offered at various locations nationwide by the military itself. Ask your local recruiter when and where you can take this test. But before you take the test, be sure to prepare for it. You need to achieve a score of 39 or higher on this test in order to be eligible for the firefighting career area. There are several test preparation books that lead you through the test step by step and give you plenty of practice taking sample tests. See Appendix B for helpful test preparation books that you can use to increase your score on the all-important ASVAB test.

The Enlistment Agreement

If you achieve a high enough score on the ASVAB test and pass all other requirements, the branch of the military you want to work in may guarantee in writing that your career area will be within the fire protection field as a part of your enlistment agreement. Be sure you read the entire enlistment agreement very carefully and ask any questions that you have before you sign it. It is a legally binding document, so don't sign it without serious thought.

You'll also need to decide the length of your enlistment before you sign on the dotted line. If you plan to leave the military to join a municipal fire department as soon as possible, then you'll want to enlist for the shortest possible time while gaining the most experience you can.

Military Training

After you enlist in the military, you'll undergo basic training for several weeks. If you have fire protection guaranteed as your career area, you'll then be given additional training as a firefighter before being assigned to a military fire department or base.

The navy offers certified apprenticeship programs for some specialties within the firefighting occupation. The air force offers a thirteen-week fire protection training program at the Goodfellow Air Force Base in San Angelo, Texas for military members who will be serving as firefighters in the marines, army, or the air force. You may be able to achieve college credit for some of your training courses from the Community College of the Air Force.

PRIVATE COMPANY FIREFIGHTER SELECTION PROCESS

Private fire companies are a growing area within the fire protection field. There are two types of private fire companies: large corporations that employ their own firefighters to protect their equipment on-site, and companies that offer fire protection service to a number of clients or in a specific geographic area. Private fire companies offer their services only when and where they are contracted by others to do so.

Companies with On-Site Firefighters

There are several large companies that hire firefighters or other fire protection specialists to work on-site to protect the company's equipment and other assets. Due to the size and high cost of the equipment at these companies, it's worth the expense of hiring an on-site crew to manage their fire prevention and suppression program. Some examples of companies that hire on-site firefighters or who contract with private fire companies to obtain on-site firefighters are the Port Columbus International Airport in Columbus, Ohio; Federal Express National Operations Center in Memphis, Tennessee; Hughes Missile System in Arizona; and Boeing, which has several locations and subsidiaries nationwide.

Here is a sample job description from a private company who is looking for a fire protection specialist:

FIRE PROTECTION SPECIALIST

Qualifications:

Prefer a four year degree in fire protection or electrical, chemical, mechanical or civil engineering. Three to five years fire protection experience with a fire protection organization or fire insurance company. Should have knowledge of governmental fire protection codes and standards, the proper handling of hazardous materials, and company policies and procedures; highly developed interpersonal and communication skills, analytical, problem solving and decision making skills.

Duties/Responsibilities:

Establish design criteria and procedures for the fire safe design and operation of new facilities, processes, and equipment. Review existing facilities, operations, and processes to assure adequate fire safety features are incorporated. Coordinate fire protection matters with appropriate organizations and maintain liaison with military, municipal, insurance and other outside agencies on fire protection engineering matters. Control and modify conditions to reduce the probabilities of fire and explosion and associated risks to personnel and property. Assure measures implemented are kept in force by proper program of inspection, test and maintenance. Salary is commensurate with qualifications and experience.

Fire Companies that Offer Fire Protection/Suppression Services

There are a growing number of private fire companies that offer fire protection and/or suppression services to other companies. One example is Rural/Metro Corporation. They select firefighters from their reserve program. In order to join their reserve program, applicants need to be at least 21 years old, possess a high school diploma or GED, pass a physical agility test, have an acceptable driving record, and pass a drug screening test and a written exam. Once applicants join the reserve program, they need to attend a fire academy on the weekends and they can begin going on fire calls after completing a certain amount of training. While firefighters are members of the reserve program, they receive minimum wage for the fire calls they go on. Graduates from the academy are granted a Firefighter II certificate. For reserve firefighters who get hired as full-time career firefighters with Rural/Metro in Arizona, their starting annual salary is approximately $35,000. Rural/Metro currently provides fire protection services to more than 25 communities and responds to more than 60,000 calls annually. Private fire companies may provide structural or wildland fire suppression and emergency services as well as airport or other special services.

How to Apply

The biggest challenge in applying for jobs with private fire companies is to find out about job openings and the names of companies that are looking for firefighters. One way is word of mouth, of course. Ask any of the firefighters or fire instructors you know if they can give you possible leads on private fire company names and locations. You might want to consider subscribing to a firefighter recruitment service that includes private fire companies in its listings (see Appendix A for contact information).

Another way to find out about these jobs is to scour your local newspapers and phone books and ask your local public librarian for information about companies that appear to have a need for fire services, such as oil refineries or ship-yards or companies in the chemical, aircraft, and aerospace industries. Once you locate such companies, call their human resources department and inquire about possible openings.

JOB OPPORTUNITIES FOR PEOPLE LEAVING THE MILITARY

There are both direct and indirect benefits for people leaving the military who are seeking firefighting positions. An indirect benefit is that firefighter training and experience in the military is highly valued. Prospective employers may look more favorably on the applications of people who have been in the military due to the high quality of firefighting training and experience those applicants received while serving in the military. The military's focus on the importance of teamwork and following orders is highly esteemed by many municipal fire chiefs. Members of the military who learn teamwork skills and who learn to follow a commander's orders while in the line of duty are considered well-equipped to do the same in a fire department; therefore, if you have a military background, it is a plus for you.

A more direct benefit occurs for select groups of people who leave the military and in some cases, their spouses. This direct benefit is normally referred to as "veteran's preference." The preference may give job applicants extra points on a portion of the testing process, ranging from 5 to 15 points. For example, if you meet the eligibility requirements, you could score a 100 on the written exam, and be given an additional 5 points due to active military duty, which would result in a score of 105. Such a high score would most likely put you at or near the top of the eligibility list for most fire departments. Many military members who served in Operation Desert Storm are eligible for this direct benefit. Specific information about who qualifies for veteran's preference should be clearly spelled out in your job application. For more information on veteran's preference programs, you can call 912-757-3000 and select *Federal Employment Topics* and then *Veterans.*

USING THE INTERNET TO HELP LAND THE JOB YOU WANT

The Internet has become a valuable resource for locating information about fire-fighting and for landing a job in this coveted field. If you don't personally have access to the Internet, don't despair because many public libraries offer free Internet access to their patrons. Don't miss out on the wealth of information available on-line. It can be worth it to check out a few local libraries if the one closest to you doesn't have Internet access. If you are attending school, check with the computer department or computer lab to see if they offer Internet access to students.

Once you enter the World Wide Web, you can access sites ranging from fire-related professional associations and bookstores to specific fire departments, recruitment agencies, and so much more. Below are key fire-related Web sites that can help maximize your chances of landing the perfect job, from giving you general information on the different careers available, to offering books for sale and bulletin boards to post questions on, to giving you inside news from experienced firefighters across the country. Check them out!

Professional Associations

Professional associations can give you general information about the fire service industry as well as specific information on a variety of topics within the field of fire protection. Check out the following Web sites for a variety of information ranging from newsletters and fire statistics to educational resources and fire news.

http://www.nfpa.org
This site contains the latest information about the National Fire Protection Association (NFPA), its departments, publications, seminars, and educational programs. The NFPA, which was organized in 1896, is the largest private organization devoted to fire protection. This site also has a good selection of links to other fire-related Web sites.

http://www.iaff.org
Web site for the International Association of Firefighters (IAFF). It offers legislative news, political actions, regulatory updates, a calendar of events, and other information of interest to firefighters.

http://www.usfa.fema.gov/
The U.S. Fire Administration (USFA) Web site offers a wealth of information about firefighting. The USFA was established by Congress in 1974, and its mission is to provide leadership, coordination, and support for the nation's fire prevention and control, fire training and education, and emergency medical services activities. This Web site offers extensive free publications on a range of firefighting topics.

http://www.afem.org/afem
Web site for the International Association of Fire Service Instructors (ISFSI). The association offers a monthly magazine. You can e-mail them at Webmaster@afem.org for more information.

http://www.nvfc.org/
Web site for the National Volunteer Fire Council, a non-profit organization. Their Web site contains news releases and other information related to volunteer firefighting. You can e-mail them at nvfcoffice@nvfc.org for more information.

http://www.wpi.edu/Academics/Depts/Fire/new-iafss/
This Web site for the International Association for Fire Safety Science (IAFSS) offers information of interest to firefighters. The association offers a newsletter, encourages the research into the science of preventing fires, holds meetings, and has an active membership.

http://www.firemarshals.org
This is a Web site for the National Association of State Fire Marshals (NASFM).

Employment Recruitment Companies

These Web sites offer employment recruiting information for a fee to prospective firefighters and to firefighters looking for promotional opportunities. Review each company carefully before you commit to subscribing to a recruitment service. Each company offers slightly different services and they all charge different fees. Recruitment companies can be especially helpful to prospective firefighters who are looking for openings in other parts of the country from which they reside. Some of these sites also contain free fire-related information at their Web sites, such as bulletin boards, bookstores, links to other sites, and chat rooms.

http://www.firecareers.com

The Perfect Firefighter Candidate is a recruitment company that offers information about job openings, filing deadlines, salary, requirements, and who to contact or how to get involved in the testing process for each job listed. You can subscribe to a monthly e-mail notification service to get job information for all levels of jobs, from firefighter to fire chief. The Web site also offers a bulletin board, chat room, and books and other products for sale. New additions are scheduled to be added to this growing Web site in the future.

http://www.psrjobs.com/fireems.htm

Public Safety Recruitment was established in 1993; it provides information from thousands of paid fire departments and EMS agencies across the nation. Their monthly newsletter, weekly e-mail service, or 900# offers prospective applicants the name of the agency recruiting and detailed information about potential jobs with contact information. Check their Web site for their latest fee schedule. They also offer an on-line bookstore where you can view descriptions of and order helpful firefighting books. You can e-mail your questions or comments to info@psrjobs.com.

http://www.firehire.com

This is a Web site for Firehire, a fire service recruitment registry. The company offers job descriptions, benefits, training information, and recruitment services for a fee to potential firefighters looking for a job.

http://www.ifpra.com

Web site of IfPRA, the International Fire & Police Recruitment Administration. The company offers recruiting information to firefighter applicants.

Books, Videos, and Other Products

Here are some Web sites that offer fire-related books, videos, audiotapes, and other products of interest to firefighters and prospective firefighters.

http://www.firebooks.com/

This site contains a firefighter's bookstore on-line. You can order a free catalog to see what books they offer or order directly from this Web site.

http://www.ifsta.org/catalog/prevention.html
A Web site for the International Fire Service Training Association (IFSTA) that offers a list of the 77 manuals they publish.

http://www.fire-police-ems.com/
Web site for FSP Books and Videos, a company that sells books, videos, and other materials related to fire, police, and EMS. You can place orders directly from this site.

Wildland Firefighter Information

These Web sites offer information useful for prospective or active wildfire firefighters on the state or federal level.

http://www.nifc.gov/
The National Interagency Fire Center (NIFC), in Boise, Idaho, includes the nation's primary logistical support center for wildland fire suppression. Working with state and local agencies, NIFC provides national response to wildfires and other emergencies and serves as a focal point for wildland fire information and technology.

http://www.blm.gov:80/careers/employ5.html
This Bureau of Land Management Web site discusses how to obtain federal firefighting jobs and offers a list of state agencies with contact information.

http://www.jobsfed.com
If you are looking for a wildland firefighting job from the federal government, you might want to check out this Web site. Select *Live Jobs*, then *Law Enforcement/Fire*, and then *Fire Protection and Prevention* to see a list of federal fire-related job postings.

http://www.usajobs.opm.gov
This Web site includes federal wildland firefighting job opportunities. It is a service provided by the Office of Personnel Management (OPM).

http://www.neotecinc.com/wildfire/
This is the Web site of *Wildfire* magazine, which is published by the International Association of Wildland Fire. This magazine discusses wildland fire safety and

current issues in wildland fire and is written by fire fighters, fire managers, and experts in aviation and crew resource management.

Other Fire-Related Web Sites

Here are a variety of Web sites that contain information related to firefighting. You can look for job leads, keep up with industry changes, look for networking contacts, and stay abreast of fire-related news by accessing these sites on a regular basis.

http://www.rescue1.com/fire411.htm

Rescue One offers a Web site containing information related to EMS, Police, and Fire occupations. The address listed above links you directly to the fire headquarters page, which contains a list of over 30 links to other fire-related Web sites, including links to specific fire departments across the nation, recruitment companies, federal and state government agencies, professional associations, and fire reports.

http://www.ci.la.ca.us/dept/PER/lafd.htm

This City of Los Angeles Fire Recruitment Web site discusses their application process and minimum requirements for becoming a firefighter in L.A. To get an application from them, you can call 212-847-LAFD. You can access their 24-hour job hotline by calling 213-847-9424.

http://www.firefighting.com

This is an interactive Web site that offers news, press releases, and products. Current firefighters are invited to post information and news on the site.

http://www.firetv.com

This site offers press releases and news stories related to firefighting.

http://www.fstc.com

Fire Service Testing Company, Inc. has a Web site that offers information about fire and emergency service personnel testing for entrance and promotional exams. Services include written tests, test software, question banks, and assessments. Online practice tests are available for a fee.

THE INSIDE TRACK

Who:	Floyd Virgil
What:	Military Firefighter
Where:	Keesler Air Force Base, Biloxi, Mississippi
How long:	Five years in the Keesler Air Force Base; almost 20 years as a military firefighter

Insider's Advice:

Think long and hard before you decide on a firefighting career in the military. You have to really want to do it and feel very strongly about it, otherwise it may not be the job for you. Don't take it lightly; think it through. The job can be hard on your family life, due to family separation and the 24 hour on, 24 hour off work schedule. On the other hand, the job can be very rewarding if you really love your job. I was able to work in England and Japan during my career, so my three boys got a chance to grow up in some very exciting places and learn a lot of different things that they would never have been able to do if I hadn't been in the military fire service.

If you do decide you want a firefighting career in the military, try to get a guaranteed job offer on your contract when you first come in. That's what I did, so I knew that I would get a job as a firefighter in the air force before I joined up. If recruiters don't still offer that feature, at least apply for firefighting training as soon as you can after you get into basic training.

Insider's Take on the Future:

I'm planning to retire in about 90 days! By that time, I will have 20 years in the military and that's the minimum requirement for retiring. You also have to have earned certain grade levels or ranks by the time you want to retire, which I have done. I'm planning to get hired by a nearby municipal airport firefighting crew after I retire from the military service.

CHAPTER | 3

This chapter describes the different types of fire-related training programs that are available. You'll see sample courses and get the inside scoop on training programs across the country. Then you'll find a directory of close to 500 schools that offer fire-related training programs.

FIRE SCIENCE TRAINING PROGRAMS

The growing need for increased education in order to land a firefighting job cannot be ignored. While the published minimum requirements listed for getting a job as a career firefighter are often a high school diploma or its equivalent, the reality is that the vast majority of successful firefighter applicants possess significantly more education than that. Many applicants have completed a fire science certificate or associate degree and several have also obtained EMT training and certification in order to successfully land a job in this highly competitive field.

All the firefighters interviewed for this book confirm that applicants with more education and training is the emerging trend in fire departments around the nation. Check with your local fire departments to find out what type of training job applicants have in your area. You'll also need to find out if firefighter and/or EMT certification are needed to get hired as a municipal firefighter in your state. For example, in Florida, all job applicants must obtain Firefighter I and EMT certification *before* they can be hired by a municipal fire department. On the other hand, in many states, you may obtain certification after you are hired.

TYPES OF TRAINING COURSES

You can take several different routes to getting the firefighting training you need to compete successfully for a paid position. Below are descriptions of the major types of training programs that are available for all ages and experience levels, ranging from high school to bachelor's degrees.

Fire Explorer and Fire Cadet Programs

Depending on your age, you may be able to join a Fire Explorer program or a Fire Cadet program to get valuable firefighter training and experience. Both of these programs are offered in various locations, but not all states have both programs, so it's worth checking into to find out if your state and local area participate. Most of these programs are for people between the ages of 15-24. However, age requirements vary among programs—some cadet programs accept applicants up through age 35.

Fire Explorer Program

The Boy Scouts of America sponsor Fire Explorer programs in many locations nationwide. Through this program, people (referred to as *explorers*) between the ages of 15 and 21 can learn about every aspect of firefighting by working with an affiliated fire department. In many cases, explorers are allowed to respond to calls and ride along as observers. While explorers are trained in fire suppression, they are not allowed to go into a burning building. There are, however, numerous tasks that supervised explorers can do outside of a fire, which firefighters inside the building rely upon.

You can get information about the Fire Explorer program by contacting the Boy Scouts of America, Fire Exploring Program, P.O. Box 152079, Irving, Texas, 75015, or by contacting your local fire department to see if it has a fire explorer program you are eligible for. Here's a list of common requirements for becoming an explorer:

* Be a citizen or live within 10 miles of the city limits
* Be between the ages of 14 -21
* Have no felony charges
* Maintain a "C" average in school
* Maintain a good standing in the community
* Have a reliable source of transportation

Fire Cadet Programs

Many municipal fire departments offer cadet programs. These programs vary among departments, but many offer training to interested parties who range in age from 18 to 35. Some cadet programs are restricted to people ages 16-21 or some other range of ages, depending on the specific department. Contact your local fire departments to find out if they sponsor cadet programs and to find out if you are eligible to apply. To give you an idea of what type of cadet programs are available, take a look at the following programs.

High School Cadets

Some fire departments offer a cadet firefighter program for high school students. These programs are designed for 16-18 year olds who wish to receive training and participate in departmental activities. Cadet members are required to have their guardian's permission to join and they normally must maintain good academic standing in high school. Members are eligible for all training, but cannot ride "in charge" until they turn 18 years old. Some fire departments recruit high school seniors under a High School Work-Study program. If you are still in high school, ask your guidance counselor for additional information about possible fire cadet programs at your school.

College Student Cadets

One example of a fire cadet college program is found in New York City. The FDNY Cadet Corps is a one-year program offered to City University of New York (CUNY) students. The Corps' goal is to establish a diverse pool of highly motivated students who train as EMTs, serve in FDNY-EMS, and will have the opportunity of taking the New York City firefighters test when it's available as a promotional exam. The Cadets spend several months participating in a rigorous course of study, undergoing extensive physical training and working closely with a team of assigned mentors. For information about the FDNY Cadet Corps program call (718) 85-CADET or (718) 694-2732/3. To see if college cadet programs are available at a college near you, call the local fire departments to inquire.

General Cadet Programs

Joining a fire cadet program is a good way to gain knowledge about a fire department, learn the basic skills of a firefighter, and get support, encouragement, and insight in pursuing a career in the fire service. Some fire departments offer hands-on emergency medical training, work experience at fire stations, and training in firefighter skills for cadets of specific ages who are enrolled in their program. The age levels vary among programs. An example of a general cadet program appears below.

Cadet Program

Cadets are required to volunteer a minimum of 24 hours every three months to the department. This may be done in a variety of areas such as teaching CPR, helping at a fire station open house, public education events, or the service van program. Cadets are responsible for staffing the service van, which provides customer service support such as non-emergency transport for behavioral health incidents. Once on-duty, cadets notify the battalion chiefs to be placed on the roll call. Field battalion chiefs and captains supervise the on-duty staff of cadets.

To be eligible for the fire cadet program, you must:

♦ Be 18-24 years of age

♦ Be an emergency medical technician (EMT) or be able to achieve certification within six months

♦ Complete an application

♦ Go through a selection board interview

♦ Get a background check

♦ Have a valid driver's license

♦ Have a good driving record

High School Preparation

If you haven't yet completed high school, you can take courses that will help you to prepare for becoming a firefighter while still in school. First of all, make sure that you have a handle on basic skills such as reading comprehension, writing, computer literacy, and basic mathematics and science. To go even further with your training, take as many of the following classes as possible:

Chemistry
Biology
Auto Mechanics
Carpentry
Drafting
Blueprint Reading
Technical Drawing
Building Construction

Physical Education (P.E.)

Computer Training

Spanish or other language

By building a strong educational foundation while still in high school, you'll increase your chances of succeeding in the next phase of your training, whether it's a certificate, a college degree, or an on-the-job training program.

Certificate Programs

There are several different types of certificates that you can get in specific training programs to help increase your chances of landing a great job. For example, many technical schools, community colleges, and other schools offer certificate programs in fire science or fire technology. You can also seek EMT certification, CPR training, or other first aid training. Some fire departments now require that all new firefighters have EMT certification prior to being hired. Check with the fire departments you're considering to find out what their specific requirements are because the requirements often differ. If you need to obtain EMT certification, take a look at the book entitled *EMT Career Starter,* published by LearningExpress to get the latest information about EMT requirements and to see an extensive directory of schools offering EMT training throughout the country.

Read all certificate materials carefully before you apply to any program of study. You should also speak to an instructor or guidance counselor at the schools you are considering to find out if the fire science certificate they offer is a good match for you. There may be several different certificates offered by one school that fall under the general heading of *Fire Science,* so you need to examine each certificate program carefully before enrolling. For example, some programs emphasize fire administration or fire inspection rather than firefighting. And some other programs may be geared for people who are already employed as firefighters but need to obtain additional certification for a promotion or to master specialized skills. So be sure to examine course materials and seek advice from someone at the school who knows exactly what each fire science certificate program is for. Most certificate programs require that applicants have a high school diploma or its equivalent before beginning the certificate program.

An example of a typical fire science certificate training program is listed below to give you an idea of what you can expect to find in a similar training program near you. This particular program is offered at a community college in

Florida. State residents pay $1,092 for full time study and $36.40 per unit for part-time study. Non-residents of Florida pay $4,068 for full-time study and $135.60 per unit for part-time study.

Certificate Program #1	
Course Name	Number of Technical Credit Hours
First Responder and Fire Terminology	2
Fire Behavior Tools and Equipment	2
Fire Hose and Fire Streams	2
Fire Physical Fitness, Ventilation, and Salvage	2
Fire Fighting Review Course	1
Hazardous Materials and Fire Review	2
Total Credits	13

It is typical for programs to require regular attendance and an academic average of a "C" or higher to be eligible to receive a certificate upon completion of the course. Entrance requirements may include a physical ability exam and a medical exam.

Certificate degree programs vary in content and length depending on what school and state you are in. For instance, take a look at the certificate program in fire science that is shown below. This one is offered at a community college in California and is much longer than the one listed above that is in Florida. This certificate program requires a total of 43 units (or credit hours). The tuition for California residents is free; residents pay approximately $410 in fees per year. The tuition for non-residents of California is $3,510 annually for full-time study and $117 per unit for part-time study.

Certificate Program #2	
Course Name	Number of Credit Hours
Introduction to Fire Technology	3
Fundamentals of Fire Behavior and Control	3
Fundamentals of Fire Prevention	3
Fundamentals of Personal Safety and Emergency Action	3
Fire Fighting Tactics and Strategy	3
Hazardous Materials I and II	6
Applied Chemistry	3
Fire Protection Equipment and Systems	3
Fundamentals of Fire Protection	3
Building Construction for Fire Protection	3
Fire Investigation	3
Electives	7
Total Credits	43

Associate Degree Programs

An associate degree program's length of study is two academic or two calendar years. Entrance requirements include a high school diploma or a GED, and some programs require college prep courses to be taken in high school. Many associate degree programs require entrance and placement exams. An associate degree program differs from a certificate program in that some courses are taken in liberal arts along with the courses that are required for your major. Courses in your major combine classroom theory with practical application of the skills you need.

Read all college materials carefully before you apply to an associate degree program. You should also speak to an instructor or guidance counselor at the school you are considering to find out if the fire science associate degree it offers is a good match for you. There may be several different specialties offered by one school that fall under the general heading of *Fire Science*, so you need to examine each associate degree program carefully before enrolling. For example, some degree programs emphasize fire administration or fire protection engineering rather than firefighting. Other programs are designed for people who are already employed as firefighters and are seeking additional training to prepare for a promotion or otherwise further their career. Some associate degree programs combine both pre-employment students and post-employment students in the same class, so you could be studying alongside several career firefighters in one or more of your courses. If that's the case, take the opportunity to get to know them and ask lots of questions so you'll be better prepared when you enter the job-hunting phase. A community college guidance counselor from Georgia says:

> Our associate degree program is made up of both career firefighters and people who want to become career firefighters. The courses are designed so each of these two groups can benefit from them. While our program is geared more for fire lieutenants and other firefighters, we always have a number of aspiring firefighters who enroll and who benefit from the courses.

A typical associate degree training program is listed below to give you an idea of what you can expect to find in a similar training program near you. This is a program that leads to an Associate of Applied Science Degree in Fire Science Technology with a concentration in Fire Suppression at a technical community college in Tennessee. The program is designed to serve the needs of students in the fire service, and to prepare others to enter this service. The total number of credit hours needed to complete the degree is 66. State residents pay $1,563 tuition per year for full-time study and $44 per unit for part-time study. Non-residents of Tennessee pay $5,880 tuition per year for full-time study and $172 per unit for part-time study.

Associate of Applied Science Degree

First Year Course Names:	Number of Credit Hours
Computer Literacy	3
Composition I	3
Introduction to Fire Science	3
Building Construction for Fire Science	3
Fire Apparatus and Equipment	3
Fire Fighting Tactics and Strategy I	3
Fire Fighting Tactics and Strategy II	3
Fundamentals of Public Speaking	3
Humanities Elective	3
Fire Science Electives	6
Mathematics Elective	3

Second Year Course Names:	Number of Credit Hours
Fire Supervision and Community Relations	3
Principles of Fire Protection Chemistry or Chemistry of Hazardous Materials	4
Fundamentals of Emergency Service Safety	3
Fire Inspection Principles	3
State and Local Government or Introduction to American Government	3
Psychology of Personal Adjustment or General Psychology I	3
Fire Science Electives	6
Natural Science Elective	4
Unrestricted Elective	1
Total Credits	66

Bachelor's Degree Programs

The bachelor's degree program combines major courses with general education in a four-year curriculum in a college or university setting. You may be admitted to your major program as a freshman or after one or two years of general education or liberal arts courses at another institution. The bachelor of science degree with a major in Fire Protection Engineering or Fire Science Management is normally pursued by people who are planning a career in fire protection engineering or who are planning to advance their career in the fire services. Therefore, if you want to land an entry-level position as a firefighter, you may not want to take this route.

However, it's a highly personal choice to decide what training program is right for you, so don't be put off from getting a fire-related bachelor's degree just because most entry-level firefighters don't have one. If you plan to advance in your career up to the level of fire chief, a bachelor's degree in fire science would be a big plus. Also, if you would prefer working as a fire protection engineer instead of as a firefighter, then you would need to pursue a fire protection bachelor's degree. See below for some examples of courses you might take for a bachelor's degree in fire protection engineering. This list does not include all the courses required for a bachelor's degree, but will give you an idea of what to expect. These courses are offered at a major university in Maryland where annual tuition is $4,460 for state residents and $10,589 for non-residents.

Fire Protection Engineer	
Linear Algebra	Calculus
Differential Equations	General Physics I, and II
Fire Dynamics	Mechanics of Materials
Introduction to Fire Protection Engineering	
Computer Applications	Fire Alarm and Special Hazards Design
Fire Protection Systems Design I	Fire Protection Fluid Mechanics
Pyrometrics of Materials	Heat Transfer Applications in Fire Protection
Thermodynamics	Mechanics of Deformable Solids
Fire Protection Hazard Analysis	Principles of Electrical Engineering
	Life Safety and Risk Analysis

The entrance requirements are more competitive for a bachelor's degree program than for shorter training programs. A high school diploma or its equivalent (GED) is required for admission, and placement exams, satisfactory SAT and ACT scores, a high-quality writing sample, positive references, and an acceptable high school GPA may also be required.

Some firefighters obtain an associate degree in fire science and then pursue a bachelor's degree in fire science through distance learning (see section below entitled *Distance Training Programs* for more information about these programs).

Fire Academies

While many states have state-sponsored or private fire academies to train new municipal firefighters, these academies are normally for employed firefighters only. So if you come across a listing for a fire academy that offers Firefighter I certification, be sure to call the academy to see if they admit anyone who is not currently an employed firefighter. There may be a few exceptions to the rule as to who will allow prospective firefighters into their fire academy, but it would be rare indeed. However, if a fire academy is affiliated with a community college, then prospective firefighters are normally able to enter the program. Again, requirements vary among states, so check carefully what the entrance requirements are for any fire academies you find.

Distance Training Programs

A growing number of programs are available that are designed for students to earn a degree in fire science while working full or part time. Better yet, you never have to go to class! Several colleges and universities now have programs with names like *Degrees at a Distance, Correspondence Courses,* or *Long Distance Learning* that allow you to study and take courses on your own, without attending formal classes.

Distance learning is basically independent study. It focuses on the idea that adults, through their jobs, personal activities, and general life experience, have many of the tools necessary to be successful, independent learners. Generally they have organizational and time management skills, basic writing and communication skills, and lots of motivation and initiative, and they tend to make serious commitments to their education. If you already have some work and life experience behind you, and believe you are a good candidate for independent study, this could be an excellent way to get the fire service education you need. This also can be a good option for working firefighters to complete their bachelor's degrees, if desired. Check with the schools you're interested in to find out if they offer any fire-related distance learning programs. You can also check Appendix B for books about distance learning programs.

National Fire Academy's Degrees at a Distance Program

A specific program you might want to check out is the Open Learning Fire Service Program (OLFSP). This nationwide independent study program is sponsored by the National Fire Academy and is offered by a consortium of accredited colleges and universities, each of which serves specific states in a given geographical region.

Its course offerings are at the college junior and senior level. Through the OLFSP, you can take individual courses for credit to upgrade your professional skills; earn a certificate from the National Fire Academy for successfully completing six courses; or complete the entire curriculum and turn a two-year Associate degree into a four-year Bachelor's degree. (See the accompanying sidebar and the list of participating schools that appears at the end of the directory in this chapter.)

The OLFSP's 12-course curriculum is designed to supplement each participating institution's requirements for a Bachelor's degree. Like traditional college courses, these programs include plenty of reading assignments, written exercises, and exams. And just because students don't go to actual classes doesn't mean they don't have meaningful contact with qualified instructors. Most students have conferences with instructors by telephone, and some programs offer the opportunity to communicate with instructors, other students, and fire service professionals over a computer network as well.

Learning the OLSFP Way

Courses offered through the Open Learning Fire Service Program (OLFSP) cover a full range of topics important to firefighters and other fire service professionals—from fire science to administration to prevention technology. Although the OLFSP curriculum is aimed at the junior-senior level, its course listing below is representative of the types of classes you can sign up for in traditional (non-independent study) college programs at different academic levels.

- Fire Dynamics
- Police and Legal Foundations of Fire Protection
- The Community and Fire Threat
- Applications of Fire Research
- Incendiary Fire Analysis and Investigation
- Fire Protection Structure and Systems Design
- Fire-related Human Behavior
- Fire Prevention Organization and Management
- Analytic Approaches to Public Fire Protection
- Personnel Management for the Fire Service
- Advanced Fire Administration
- Disaster and Fire Defense Planning
- Managerial Issues in Hazardous Materials

You can contact participating colleges/universities directly for more information: addresses, phone numbers, contact names for individual schools, and a list of the states served by each, are provided at the end of this chapter's directory. Or you can contact the program's main sponsor, the National Fire Academy, at the following address: Federal Emergency Management Agency, U. S. Fire Administration, National Fire Academy, Open Learning Fire Service Program, 16825 South Seton Avenue, Emmitsburg, MD 21727.

HOW TO CHOOSE THE TRAINING PROGRAM THAT'S BEST FOR YOU

Since there are so many different training programs, it can be a challenge to find the one that is best for you. The first step is to find out what schools are near you that offer fire science training or other college courses that will help you land a career firefighter job. Check the directory in the second half of this chapter to find a list of schools that offer fire-related training programs nationwide.

The next step is to contact the schools that are in your location to find out more information. You should always confirm that they currently offer courses that are related to fire services. Ask to speak to a guidance counselor or to someone in the fire science or fire technology department to get detailed information about the fire science programs offered. Request a school catalog and whatever brochures that are available about the school and its programs. Read these documents carefully when you receive them, especially the fine print in the college catalog. You want to find out exactly what courses are required for your program, how much it will cost, and how long the program will last.

Another thing you can do, if you have the time, is to visit the schools in your area and talk to a guidance counselor in person at each one. These counselors are trained to help you identify your needs and decide if their school will meet those needs. Follow these steps when preparing for an on-campus visit:

- Contact the office of admissions to request an appointment to visit. Remember to ask for the name of the person making the appointment and the person you will be meeting with. Try to schedule a meeting with an instructor in the fire science program as well as a guidance counselor in the admissions or counseling department.
- Bring a copy of your transcript or permanent record card if you will have the opportunity to meet with an admissions counselor during your visit.
- Include a list of honors or awards you have received in high school or the community, including documentation of any volunteer or fire cadet training.
- Ask to tour the fire science practical experience area, if available. This tour should show you the available equipment and materials for simulations and other fire exercises. Many schools are affiliated with one or more local fire departments or private fire academies, so they offer this hands-on training through another agency.

Be prepared to ask questions about the school and surrounding community, including extracurricular activities, work opportunities, and anything else you don't find explained in the promotional brochures.

Asking the Right Questions

After you visit several schools and narrow your choices down to two or three schools, the next step is to ask tough questions about each program to make the final selection. Here are some important questions you should ask about a prospective school to see if it measures up to your standards. After each question, you'll find sample answers that you should receive or other considerations that you should think about before choosing a particular school.

Does the Fire Science or Fire Technology program admit students who are not currently full-time paid firefighters?

You need to find out if the school you are considering allows people who are not yet career firefighters to enter the program. This is an important question to ask as a first step in evaluating a school's program. Answers to this question will vary immensely depending on what school you're considering because of the variety of programs and affiliations each school has with local fire departments and county, state, or federal regulations. Years ago, most fire science degree programs were aimed at career firefighters who wanted to get promoted or move into a specialized area in the fire service.

However, things have changed greatly over the years. Due to the competitive nature of landing a job as a career firefighter in today's tight market, many more associate degree and certificate programs are available to help people gain the firefighting knowledge and experience that will set them above the crowd.

Some schools advertise that they are geared to helping students learn all they can about firefighting and want to help students prepare for landing a great job upon graduation. Other schools may allow only career firefighters who are working full time at a local fire department into their program. Some schools may allow you to enter their program if you're a volunteer firefighter. Still other schools allow a mixture of students to take fire science programs. In that case, you'll be studying alongside career firefighters as well as other aspiring firefighters like yourself.

Depending on the requirements in your county or state, you may need to enroll in a certificate training program (rather than an associate degree program) in order to pass the state's examination and certification process. This is currently the standard procedure in Florida, for example. Schools also have different programs of study and different areas of specialization, such as fire protection engineering or technology, fire administration, firefighting, fire technology, and fire inspection in addition to or under the heading of fire science.

Therefore, you need to contact each school you are considering and ask to speak to an instructor or a representative of the fire science or fire technology program. Ask specifically if you can enroll in their fire science program with your background and credentials, and find out what type of students they admit for each program to see if a certificate or associate degree program would be best for you. Even if you can't enroll in a program as a degree-seeking student, you may be able to take selected courses on an audit basis. It doesn't hurt to ask, and any fire-related courses that you take can only improve your chances of landing your first job.

What requirements will I need to attend?

Check with each school you are considering to find out what its specific entrance requirements are. Requirements vary from school to school. For instance, you may be required to do any one or more of the following:

* Take English, math, or science placement tests
* Take and achieve a certain score on the SAT or ACT if you have not already taken them in high school
* Have a certain level GPA from high school
* Take a physical exam
* Take a physical ability test

If you feel that you won't have any trouble meeting the entrance requirements for your targeted schools, then you're all set. If one of the schools you are considering has an entrance requirement that you think you may not meet, call an admissions counselor and discuss your particular case with her or him. Most schools will at least offer some type of remedial help if needed, so students can meet the requirement in the future.

What are the qualifications of the faculty?

There should be some faculty members with degrees in fire science (bachelor's or master's degree in fire science or a related area) and/or faculty members who have extensive experience as firefighters and firefighter instructors. The faculty should be accessible to students for conferences.

Is the school accredited?

It's important that the school you choose be accredited. Accreditation is a rigorous and complex process that ensures sound educational and ethical business practices at the schools that achieve accreditation. It's a process schools undergo voluntarily.

Some accrediting agencies are national and some are regional. The name of the accrediting agency for the school you're interested in will probably be plainly printed on the school's general catalog because schools are usually proud of their accredited status. If you can't locate the information in a school's printed materials, you can make sure of their status by calling the school and asking for the name(s) of its accrediting agency or agencies.

An important point to remember is that, if the school you choose is not accredited, you cannot get financial aid through any of the government programs. (See chapter four for more information about how to obtain financial aid.)

Does the school have access to the latest firefighting equipment and technology?

It's a good idea when you are visiting schools—and you should definitely visit the schools you're seriously considering—to ask to see their fire service training equipment. Current firefighting technology and training should be available to students. The hands-on portion of the training program should cover basic firefighting principles and should offer simulation exercises to practice the basic skills needed for a firefighter, such as:

- Fire Hose Techniques
- Extinguishing fires in test modules
- How to move while wearing heavy equipment
- Working in smoke-filled rooms
- Pump operations
- Confined space rescue

What will the program cost?

Tuition varies according to many factors, but especially according to the length of the program and the area in which the school is located. Often, tuition costs also depend on if you are a resident of the state in which you are applying for school. You should sit down and figure out how much each program that you are considering will cost. If the tuition is not listed in the college's course catalog, call the school and ask what its current resident and non-resident rates are (whichever applies to you). As you can see from the sample tuition costs listed in the sample programs above (certificate, associate, and bachelor's), there is quite a range of costs for completing a training program.

Don't forget to include the following items when figuring out how much each school will cost: books, admission fees, lab fees, rent, transportation, child care. If one school is located near where you live, you may be able to save money on parking and gasoline by walking or taking a bus. Perhaps one school has lower-priced child care or cheaper admission fees. After you create an estimate of the total costs for each school you are considering, you'll be armed with one more item that can make or break a school's desirability for you.

What is the student-teacher ratio?

The student-teacher ratio is a statistic that shows the average number of students assigned to one teacher in a classroom or lab. It's important that the student-teacher ratio not be too high. Education suffers if classrooms are too crowded, or if a teacher has too many students to be able to see everyone who wishes to be seen for a private conference. According to one of the top national accrediting agencies—the Accrediting Council for Independent Colleges and Schools—a reasonable student-teacher ratio for skills training is 30 students to 1 teacher in a lecture setting and 15 students to 1 teacher in a laboratory or clinical instruction setting. At very good schools the ratio is even better than the ACICS recommends.

When are classes scheduled?

Find out if the school you're considering offers any weekend or evening classes. If you need to work full time during regular business hours while attending school, you'll need to find a school that offers classes at non-traditional times.

Is the campus environment suitable?

When you visit the school, determine how the campus feels to you. Is it too big? Too small? Too quiet? Is the campus in a bustling city or rural community? Is it easily accessible? Do you need to rely on public transportation to get there? Select a school that has a campus environment that meets your needs.

Does the school offer child care facilities?

This may or may not be of concern to you. If it is, you'll want to tour the child care facilities and interview the people who work in the child care center to see if the care is suitable for your children.

> ## Application Tips from Admissions Directors
>
> ♦ Apply as early as you can. You'll need to fill out an application and submit high school or GED transcripts and any copies of SAT, ACT, or other test scores used for admission. If you haven't taken these tests, you may have to before you can be admitted. Call the school and find out when the next program starts, then apply at least a month or two prior to make sure you can complete requirements before the program begins.
>
> ♦ You may receive a pre-written request for high school transcripts from the admissions office when you get your application. Make sure you send those requests as soon as possible, so the admissions process is not held up in any way.
>
> ♦ Make an appointment as soon as possible to take any placement tests that may be required.
>
> ♦ Pay your fees before the deadline. Enrollment is not complete each quarter or semester until students have paid all fees by the date specified on their registration form. If fees are not paid by the deadline, their classes may be canceled. If you are going to receive financial aid, apply as early as you can.
>
> ♦ Find out early in the application process if you must pass a physical or have any other medical history forms on file for the school you choose, so this does not hold up your admission.

DIRECTORY OF FIRE-RELATED TRAINING PROGRAMS

This section provides a representative listing of schools in each state that offer fire-related training programs. These programs offer a range of training choices—from certificate to associate and bachelor's degrees—and include fire science, fire technology, fire protection engineering, fire administration, and fire protection technology programs. The schools are listed in alphabetical order by city in each state, so you can quickly locate schools that are near you. All programs provide school name, address, and phone number, so you can contact each school directly to get more information and application forms from the schools that interest you. At the end of the directory, you'll find a separate list of seven schools that participate in the Open Learning Fire Science Program (OLFSP), including the list of states that each school serves. For more information on the OLFSP program, see the section earlier in this chapter entitled *Distance Training Programs*.

This listing is intended to help you begin your search for an appropriate school. The specific schools included in this listing, however, are not endorsed or recommended by LearningExpress. Always contact the schools you are considering to get current information on program requirements and areas of specialization before you apply.

ALABAMA

Lurleen B. Wallace State Junior College
P.O. Box 1418
Andalusia 36420
205-222-6591

James H. Faulkner State Community
College
1900 U.S. Highway 31 South
Bay Minette 36507-2619
334-580-2134

Jefferson State Community College
2601 Carson Road
Birmingham 35215-3098
205-853-1200

Lawson State Community College
3060 Wilson Road SW
Birmingham 35221-1798
205-925-2515

Snead State Community College
Boaz 35957
205-593-5120

John C. Calhoun State Community
College
P.O. Box 2216
Decatur 35609-2216
205-306-2500

Gadsden State Community College
1001 George Wallace Drive
Gadsden 35901-0227
205-549-8200

Wallace State Community College
P.O. Box 2000
Hanceville 35077-2000
205-352-6403

Community College of the Air Force
Maxwell Air Force Base 36112-6613
334-953-6436

Bishop State Community College
351 North Broad Street
Mobile 36603-5898
334-690-6419

Alabama Southern Community College
Monroeville 36460
334-575-3156

Northwest-Shoals Community College
P.O. Box 2545
Muscle Shoals 35662
205-331-6218

Northwest Alabama Community
College
Route 3, Box 77
Phil Campbell 35581
205-993-5331

Chattahoochee Valley State Community
College
119 Broad Street
Phoenix City 36969-7928
334-291-4928

George Corley Wallace State
Community College
3000 Earl Goodwin Parkway
Selma 36702-1049
334-875-2634

Shelton State Community College
1301 15th Street East
Tuscaloosa 35404
205-759-1541

Southern Union State Community
College
Roberts Street
Wadley 36276
205-395-2211

ALASKA

Community and Technical College
University of Alaska
3211 Providence Drive
Anchorage 99508-8306
907-786-6400

University of Alaska
Tanana Valley Campus
510 Second Avenue
Fairbanks 99701
907-474-7400

University of Alaska Anchorage
Matanuska-Susitna College
P.O. Box 2889
Palmer 99645-2889
907-745-9726

ARIZONA

Cochise College
Douglas 85607-9724
520-364-0336

Coconino County Community College
3000 North 4th Street
Flagstaff 86003
520-527-1222

Glendale Community College
6000 West Olive Avenue
Glendale 85302-3090
602-435-3305

Northland Pioneer College
203 West Hopi Drive
Holbrook 86025-0610
520-524-1993

Mohave Community College
1971 Jagerson Avenue
Kingman 86401-1299
520-757-0847

Estrella Mountain Community College
3000 North Dysart Road
Litchfield Park 85340
602-932-8000

Mesa Community College
1833 West Southern Avenue
Mesa 85202-4866
602-461-7478

Phoenix College
1202 West Thomas Road
Phoenix 85013-4234
602-285-7500

Rio Salado Community College
640 North 1st Avenue
Phoenix 85003
602-223-4000

Yavapai College
1100 East Sheldon Street
Prescott 86301-3297
520-776-2158

Scottsdale Community College
9000 East Chaparral Road
Scottsdale 85250-2699
602-423-6100

Cochise College-Sierra Vista Campus
Sierra Vista 85635-2317
520-515-5412

Pima County Community College
2202 West Anklam Road
Tucson 85706
520-206-6640

Arizona Western College
P.O. Box 929
Yuma 85366
602-726-1050

ARKANSAS

Southern Arkansas University Tech
Camden 71701
501-574-4504

Cossatot Community College
P.O. Box 960
DeQueen 71832
501-584-4471

Garland County Community College
101 College Drive
Hot Springs 71913-9174
501-767-9371

Shorter College
604 Locust Street
North Little Rock 72114-4885
501-374-6305

Black River Technical College
1416 Highway 304 East
Pocahontas 72455
501-892-4565

CALIFORNIA
Cabrillo College
6500 Soquel Drive
Aptos 95003-3194
408-479-6201

Bakersfield College
1801 Panorama Drive
Bakersfield 93305-1299
805-395-4301

Barstow Community College
2700 Barstow Road
Barstow 92311-6699
619-252-2411

University of California
Fire Safety Engineering Science
Davis Hall
Berkeley 94720
510-643-8415

Palo Verde College
811 West Chanslor Way
Blythe 92225-1118
619-922-6168

Southwestern College
900 Otay Lakes Road
Chula Vista 91910
619-421-6700

Columbia College
P.O. Box 1849
Columbia 95310
209-533-5100

Compton Community College
1111 East Artesia Blvd.
Compton 90221-5393
310-637-2660

Fresno City College
1101 East University Avenue
Fresno 93741-0002
209-442-4600

Glendale Community College
1500 North Verdugo Road
Glendale 91208-2894
818-240-1000

Chabot College
25555 Hesperian Blvd.
Hayward 94545-5001
510-786-6700

Imperial Valley College
P.O. Box 158
Highway 111 and Aten Road
Imperial 92251-0158
619-352-8320

College of the Desert
Copper Mountain Campus
P.O. Box 1398
Joshua Tree 92252
619-366-3791

College of Marin
835 College Avenue
Kentfield 94904
415-485-9417

Antelope Valley College
3041 W. Avenue K
Lancaster 93536-5426
805-943-3241

Las Positas College
3033 Collier Canyon Road
Livermore 94550-7650
510-373-5800

Long Beach City College
4901 East Carson Street
Long Beach 90808-1780
310-938-4353

California State University
Department of Industrial Studies
5151 University Drive
Los Angeles 90032-8530
213-343-3000

Yuba College
2088 North Beale Road
Marysville 95901-7699
916-741-6720

Merced College
3600 M Street
Merced 95348-2898
209-384-6190

Modesto Junior College
435 College Avenue
Modesto 95350-5800
209-575-6498

Monterey Peninsula College
980 Fremont Street
Monterey 93940-4799
408-646-4006

East Los Angeles College
1301 Avenida Cesaer Chavez
Monterey Park 91754-6001
213-265-8650

Merritt College
12500 Campus Drive
Oakland 94619-3196
510-436-2598

Butte Community College
3536 Butte Campus Drive
Oroville 95965-8399
916-895-2511

Oxnard College
4000 South Rose Avenue
Oxnard 93033-6699
805-488-0911

College of the Desert
43500 Monterey Avenue
Palm Desert 92260-9305
760-773-2519

Pasadena City College
1570 East Colorado Blvd.
Pasadena 91106
818-585-7123

Los Medanos College
2700 East Leland Road
Pittsburg 94565-5197
510-253-4254

Porterville College
100 East College Avenue
Porterville 93257-6058
209-791-2200

Shasta College
1065 North Old Oregon Trail
Redding 96049-6006
916-225-4841

Cerro Coso Community College
College Heights Blvd.
Ridgecrest 93555-9571
760-389-6201

Riverside Community College
4800 Magnolia Avenue
Riverside 92506-1293
909-222-8615

Sierra Community College
5000 Rocklin Road
Rocklin 95677-3397
916-781-0430

American River College
4700 College Oak Drive
Sacramento 95841-4286
916-484-8261

Cosumnes River College
8401 Center Parkway
Sacramento 95823-5799
916-688-7410

Hartnell College
156 Homestead Avenue
Salinas 93901-1697
408-755-6711

San Diego Miramar College
10440 Black Mountain Road
San Diego 92126-2999
619-536-7800

City College of San Francisco
50 Phelan Avenue
San Francisco 94112-1821
415-239-3000

Mount San Jacinto College
21400 Highway 79
San Jacinto 92383-2399
909-487-6752

Palomar Community College
1140 West Mission Road
San Marcos 92069-1487
619-744-1150

College of San Mateo
1700 West Hillsdale Blvd.
San Mateo 94402-3784
415-574-6165

Rancho Santiago College
1530 West 17th Street
Santa Anna 92706-3398
714-564-6000

Mission College
3000 Mission College Blvd.
Santa Clara 95054-1897
408-748-2700

Allan Hancock College
800 South College Drive
Santa Maria 93454-6399
805-922-6966

Santa Monica College
1900 Pico Blvd.
Santa Monica 90405-1644
310-450-5150

Santa Rosa Junior College
1501 Mendocino Avenue
Santa Rosa 95401-4395
707-527-4011

Columbia College
11600 Columbia College Drive
Sonora 95370
209-588-5231

Lake Tahoe Community College
1 College Drive
South Lake Tahoe 96150-4524
916-541-4660

San Joaquin Delta Community College
5151 Pacific Avenue
Stockton 95207-6370
209-474-5615

Solano Community College
P.O. Box 246
Suisun City 94585-3197
707-864-7171

Cogswell College
1175 Bordeaux Drive
Sunnyville 94089-1299
408-541-0100

El Camino College
16007 Crenshaw Blvd.
Torrance 90506-0001
310-660-3418

Los Angeles Valley College
5800 Fulton Avenue
Van Nuys 91401-4096
818-781-1200

Victor Valley College
18422 Bear Valley Road
Victorville 92392-5849
619-245-4271

College of Sequoias
915 South Mooney Blvd.
Visalia 93277-2234
209-730-3727

Mount San Antonio College
1100 North Grand Avenue
Walnut 91789-1399
909-594-5611

College of the Siskiyous
800 College Avenue
Weed 96094-2899
916-938-5215

Rio Hondo College
3600 Workman Mill Road
Whittier 90601-1699
562-692-0921

Los Angeles Harbor College
1111 South Figueroa Place
Wilmington 90744-2311
310-522-8214

Crafton Hills College
11711 Sand Canyon Road
Yucaipa 92399-1799
909-389-3372

COLORADO
Community College of Aurora
16000 East Centretech Parkway
Aurora 80011
303-360-4792

Pikes Peak Community College
5675 South Academy Blvd.
Colorado Springs 80906-5498
719-540-7147

Colorado Mountain College
Spring Valley Campus
3000 County Road 114
Glenwood Springs 81601
970-945-7481

Aims Community College
P.O. Box 69
Greeley 80632-0069
970-330-8008

Red Rocks Community College
13300 West 6th Avenue
Lakewood 80228-1255
303-988-6160

Arapahoe Community College
2500 West College Drive
P.O. Box 9002
Littleton 80160-9002
303-797-5900

CONNECTICUT
Eli Whitney Regional Vocational School
71 Jones Road
Hamden 06514
203-397-4045

Hartford State Technical College
401 Flatbush Avenue
Hartford 06106
203-520-7800

Gateway Community Technical College
60 Sargent Drive
New Haven 06511
203-789-7043

Charter Oak State College
Newington 06111-2646
860-666-4595

Norwalk State Technical College
188 Richards Avenue
Norwalk 06854-1655
203-857-7060

Thames Valley State Technical College
547 New London Turnpike
Norwich 06360
203-886-0177

Three Rivers Community Technical
College
574 New London Turnpike
Mahan Drive
Norwich 06360
203-886-1931

Naugatuack Valley Community
Technical College
750 Chase Parkway
Waterbury 06708-3000
203-575-8078

University of New Haven
Fire Science Department
300 Orange Avenue
West Haven 06516-1916
203-932-7088

DELAWARE
Delaware Technical & Community
College
Stanton Campus
P.O. Box 1260
Newark 19713
302-571-5366

DISTRICT OF COLUMBIA
University of the District of Columbia
4200 Connecticut Avenue NW
Washington 20008-1175
202-274-5010

FLORIDA
South Tech Education Center
1300 Southwest 30th Avenue
Boynton Beach 33426-9099
407-369-7000

Manatee Community College
Brandenton Campus
5840 26th Street West
Brandenton 34207-1849
813-755-1511

Brevard Community College
1519 Clear Lake Road
Cocoa 32922-6597
407-632-1111

Pasco-Hernando Community College
36727 Blanton Road
Dade City 33523-7599
813-847-2727

Wm. T. McFatter Vocational Tech Center
6500 Nova Drive
Davie 33317
954-370-8324

Daytona Beach Community College
Daytona Beach 32120
904-254-4426

Lake County Area Vocational Tech
Center
2001 Kurt Street
Eustis 32726
904-742-6486

Broward Community College
225 East Las Olas Blvd.
Fort Lauderdale 33301-2298
954-761-7464

Edison Community College
8099 College Parkway S.W.
Fort Meyers 33906-6210
941-489-9361

Indian River Community College
3209 Virginia Avenue
Fort Pierce 34981
407-462-4740

Santa Fe Community College
P.O. Box 1530
Gainesville 32606-6200
352-395-5448

Florida Junior College at Jacksonville
501 West State Street
Jacksonville 32202-4030
904-632-3110

Palm Beach Junior College
4200 Congress Avenue
Lake Worth 33461-4796
561-967-7222

Lake-Sumter Community College
Leesburg 34788-8751
352-365-3568

Chipola Junior College
3094 Indian Circle
Marianna 32446-2053
904-526-2761

Miami Dade Community College
300 N.E. Second Avenue
Miami 33132-2296
305-237-7478

James Lorenzo Walker Vocational
3702 Estey Avenue
Naples 33942-4457
941-643-0919

Central Florida Community College
P.O. Box 1388
Ocala 34478-1388
352-237-2111

Florida State Fire College
11655 NW Gainesville Road
Ocala 34482-1486
352-732-1330

Valencia Community College
P.O. Box 3028
Orlando 32802-3028
407-299-5000

St. Johns River Community College
Palatka 32177-3807
904-328-1571

Gulf Coast Community College
5230 West Highway 98
Panama City 32401-1058
904-769-1551

Naval Air Technical Training Center
Naval Air Station Pensacola
230 Chevalier Field Avenue
Pensacola 32508-5113
904-452-7212

Pensacola Junior College
Pensacola 32504-8998
904-484-1600

St. Augustine Tech Center
2980 Collins Avenue
St. Augustine 32095-9970
904-824-4401

St. Petersburg Junior College
P.O. Box 13489
St. Petersburg 33781-3489
813-341-3170

Pinellas Technical Education Center
St. Petersburg Campus
901 34th Street South
St. Petersburg 33711
813-327-3671

Seminole Community College
Highway 17-29
Sanford 32773-6199
407-328-2041

Sarasota County Technical Institute
4748 Beneva Road
Sarasota 34233
813-924-1365

Lively Technical Center
500 North Appleyard Drive
Tallahassee 32304-2895
904-487-7555

Hillsborough Community College
P.O. Box 31127
Tampa 33631
813-253-7004

Polk Community College
999 Avenue "H" N.E.
Winter Haven 33881-4299
941-297-1009

Ridge Technical Center
7700 State Road 544
Winter Haven 33881
813-299-2512

GEORGIA
Dekalb Community College
555 North Indian Creek Road
Clarkston 30021-2396
404-299-4564

Macon College
1000 College Station Drive
Macon 31206
912-471-2800

Georgia Military College
Milledgeville 31061
912-445-2707

Savannah Technical Institute
5717 White Bluff Road
Savannah 31499
912-351-4404

HAWAII
Hawaii Community College
1400 Kapiolani Street
Hilo 96720-4091
808-974-7661

Honolulu Community College
874 Dillingham Blvd.
Honolulu 96817-4598
808-845-9129

University of Hawaii
Maui Community College
Kahului 96732
808-984-3267

IDAHO
Boise State University
College of Technology
1910 University Drive
Boise 83725
208-385-3015

Eastern Idaho Tech College
1600 South 2500 East
Idaho Falls 83404-5788
208-524-3000

Lewis-Clark State College
School of Technology
500 8th Avenue
Lewiston 83501-2698
208-799-5272

Idaho State University
Fire Service Technology
P.O. Box 8054
Pocatello 82309
208-236-2123

College of Southern Idaho
315 Falls Avenue
P.O. Box 1238
Twin Falls 83303-1238
208-733-9554

ILLINOIS

Belleville Area College
2500 Carlyle Road
Belleville 62221-5899
618-235-2700

Spoon River College
Rural Route 1
Canton 61520
309-647-4645

Southern Illinois University
Carbondale Campus
Carbondale 62901-6806
618-536-4405

Parkland College
2400 West Bradley Avenue
Champaign 61821-1899
217-351-2482

City Colleges of Chicago
Harold Washington College
30 East Lake Street
Chicago 60601
312-553-6000

City Colleges of Chicago
Richard Daley College
7500 South Pulaski Road
Chicago 60652-1242
312-838-7599

Prairie State College
200 East 197th Street
P.O. Box 487
Chicago Heights 60411-8226
708-709-3516

McHenry County College
8900 U.S. Highway 14
Crystal Lake 60012-2761
815-455-8716

Danville Area Community College
Danville 61832
217-443-8775

Richland Community College
One College Park
Decatur 62521
217-875-7200

Northern Illinois University
College of Engineering
Dekalb 60115
815-753-1283

Oakton Community College
1600 East Gulf
Des Plaines 60016-1268
847-635-1703

Illinois Central College
Box 2400
East Peoria 61635-0001
309-694-5354

Metropolitan Community College
601 James R. Thompson Blvd.
East St. Louis 62201
618-482-2020

Elgin Community College
1700 Spartan Drive
Elgin 60123-7193
847-888-7385

College of DuPage
425 22nd St.
Glen Ellyn 60137
630-858-2800

Lewis and Clark Community College
Godfrey 62035-2466
618-466-3411

College of Lake County
19351 W. Washington Street
Grayslake 60030
847-223-6601

Southeastern Illinois College
3575 College Road
Harrisburg 62946
618-252-6376

Joliet Junior College
1216 Houbolt Avenue
Joliet 60431-8938
815-729-9020

Kishwaukee College
21193 Malta Road
Malta 60150
815-825-2086

Sussex Community College
College Hills
Newton 07860
201-579-5400

Illinois Valley Community College
815 North Orlando Smith Avenue
Oglesby 61348-9691
815-224-2720

William Rainey Harper College
1200 West Algonquin Road
Palatine 60067
847-925-6000

Moraine Valley Community College
10900 South 88th Avenue
Palos Hills 60465
708-974-4300

John Wood Community College
150 South 48th Street
Quincy 62301
217-224-6500

Triton College
2000 Fifth Avenue
River Grove 60171
708-456-0300

Rock Valley College
3301 North Mulford Road
Rockford 61114-5699
815-654-4286

South Suburban College
15800 South State Street
South Holland 60473
708-596-2000

Lincoln Land Community College
Shepard Road
Springfield 62794-9256
217-786-2200

Waubonsee College
Route 47 at Harter Road
Sugar Grove 60554
630-466-7900

INDIANA
Indiana Vocational Technical College
Northeast Indiana
3800 North Anthony Blvd.
Fort Wayne 46805-1430
219-480-4211

Indiana Vocational Technical College
Northwest Indiana
1440 East 35th Avenue
Gary 46409-1479
219-981-1111

Indiana Vocational Technical College
Central Indiana
1 West 26th Street
P.O. Box 1763
Indianapolis 46206-1763
317-921-4612

IOWA
Iowa State University
Fire Service Institute
Haber Road
Ames 50011-3100
515-294-6817

Des Moines Area Community College
2006 Ankeny Blvd.
Ankeny 50021
515-964-6210

Kirkwood Community College
6301 Kirkwood Blvd., SW
P.O. Box 2068
Cedar Rapids 52406-2068
319-398-5517

Iowa Western Community College
2700 College Road, Box 4-C
Council Bluffs 51502
712-325-3200

Marshalltown Community College
3700 South Center Street
Marshalltown 50158-0430
515-752-7106

Hamilton College
100 First Street Northwest
Mason City 50401
515-423-2530

Western Iowa Technical Community
College
4647 Stone Avenue
Sioux City 51106
712-274-6400

KANSAS
Dodge City Community Junior College
2501 North 14th Avenue
Dodge City 67801-2399
316-225-1321

Butler County Community Junior
College
Box 888
El Dorado 67042-3280
316-321-2222

Barton County Community College
Route 3 Box 136Z
Great Bend 67530-9283
316-792-2701

Hutchinson Community Junior College
1300 North Plum
Hutchinson 67501-5894
316-665-3536

Kansas City Kansas Community Junior
College
7250 State Avenue
Kansas City 66112-3003
913-334-1100

Johnson County Community Junior
College
12345 College Blvd. at Quivira
Overland Park 66210-1299
913-469-8500

Labette Community College
200 South 14th
Parsons 67357-4299
316-421-6700

KENTUCKY
Jefferson Community College
109 East Broadway
Louisville 40202-2005
502-584-0181

Paducah Community College
P.O. Box 7380
Paducah 42001
502-442-6131

Eastern Kentucky University
College of Law Enforcement
Richmond 40475-3101
606-622-2106

LOUISIANA
Louisiana State University
Division of Continuing Education
Baton Rouge 70803
504-769-2374

Louisiana State University at Eunice
P.O. Box 1129
Eunice 70535-1129
318-457-7311

Delgado College
501 City Park Avenue
New Orleans 70119-4399
504-483-4004

MAINE
Southern Main Vocational & Technical
Institute
2 Fort Road
South Portland 04106
207-767-9520

MARYLAND
Catonsville Community College
800 South Rolling Road
Catonsville 21228-5381
410-455-4304

University of Maryland
Dept. of Fire Protection Engineering
College Park 20472
301-314-8385

Prince George's Community College
301 Largo Road
Largo 20772
301-336-6000

Montgomery College
51 Manakee Street
Rockville 20850-1196
301-279-5036

MASSACHUSETTS
Middlesex Community College
21 Springs Road
Bedford 01730
508-656-3211

Bunker Hill Community College
250 New Rutherford Avenue
Boston 02129
617-228-2238

Massasoit Community College
290 Thatcher Street
Brockton 02402-3996
508-588-9100

North Shore Community College
1 Ferncroft Road
Danvers 01923-4093
508-762-4000

Bristol Community College
777 Elsbree Street
Fall River 02720-7395
508-678-2811

Mount Wachusett Community College
444 Green Street
Gardner 01440-1000
508-632-6600

Greenfield Community College
Greenfield 01301
413-774-3131

Northeast Maritime, Inc.
105 William Street, 3rd Fl.
New Bedford 02739-6218
508-992-4025

Anna Maria College
50 Sunset Lane
Paxton 01612-1198
508-849-3300

Berkshire Community College
West Street
Pittsfield 01201-5786
413-499-4660

Quincy College
Quincy 02169-4522
617-984-1700

Salem State College
352 Lafayette Street
Salem 01970
508-741-6200

Springfield Technical Community
College
1 Armory Square
Springfield 01105-1296
413-781-7822

Massachusetts Bay Community College
50 Oakland Street
Wellesley Hills 02181-5359
617-235-1100

Cape Cod Community College
Route 132
West Barnstable 02668-1599
508-362-2131

Quinsigamond Community College
670 West Boylston Street
Worcester 01606-2092
508-853-2300

Worcester Polytechnic Institute
Center for Fire Safety Studies
100 Institute Road
Worcester 01609-2280
508-831-5286

MICHIGAN

Washtenaw Community College
Ann Arbor 48106
313-973-3543

Oakland Community College
2900 Featherstone Road
Auburn Hills 48326
810-340-6500

Kellogg Community College
450 North Avenue
Battle Creek 49017-3397
616-965-3931

Glen Oaks Community College
62249 Shimmel Road
Centreville 49032-9719
6160-467-9945

Macomb Community College
Center Campus
44575 Garfield Road
Clinton Township 48038-1139
810-286-2228

Henry Ford Community College
5101 Evergreen Road
Dearborn 48128
313-845-9615

Southwestern Michigan College
58900 Cherry Grove Road
Dowagiac 49057
616-782-5113

Mott Community College
1401 East Court Street
Flint 48503-2089
810-762-0200

Grand Rapids Community College
143 Bostwick Avenue N.E.
Grand Rapids 49503-3201
616-771-4100

Mid-Michigan Community College
1375 South Clare Avenue
Harrison 48625-9447
517-386-6622

Kalamazoo Valley Community College
P.O. Box 4070
Kalamazoo 49003-4070
616-372-5000

Lansing Community College
419 North Capitol Avenue
Lansing 48901-7210
517-483-1252

Madonna University
36600 Schoolcraft Road
Livonia 48150
313-591-5052

Schoolcraft College
Livonia 48152-2696
313-462-4426

St. Clair County Community College
Port Huron 48061-5015
810-989-5500

Kirtland Community College
10775 North St. Helen Road
Roscommon 48653-9699
517-275-5121

Lake Superior State University
650 West Easterday Avenue
Sault Saint Marie 49783
906-635-2231

Macomb Community College
14500 Twelve Mile Road
Box 309
Warren 48093-3896
810-445-7230

Delta College
University Center 48710
517-686-9092

MINNESOTA
Lake Superior College
2101 Trinity Road
Duluth 55811
218-733-5903

Northwest Technical College
2022 Central Avenue N.E.
East Grand Forks 56721-2702
218-773-3441

Hennepin Technical College
9200 Flying Cloud Drive
Eden Prairie 56347
612-550-3134

Hibbing Community College
1515 East 25th Street
Hibbing 55746
218-262-6700

North Hennepin Community College
7411 85th Avenue North
Minneapolis 55445
612-424-0713

MISSISSIPPI
Mississippi Gulf Coast Community
College
Jefferson Davis Campus
2226 Switzer Road
Gulfport 39507
601-896-2500

Meridian Community College
910 Highway 19
Meridian 39307
601-484-8621

East Mississippi Community College
P.O. Box 158
Scooba 39358-0158
601-476-8442

MISSOURI
University of Missouri
Center for Independent Study
136 Clark Hall
Columbia 65211
800-858-6413

Jefferson College
Hillsboro 63050-2441
314-789-3951

Fort Osage Area Vocation Technical
School
2101 North Twyman Road
Independence 64058
816-650-6377

Penn Valley Community College
3201 Southwest Trafficway
Kansas City 64111
816-759-4101

Crowder College
Neosho 64850-9160
417-451-3223

Ozarks Technical Community College
1417 North Jefferson Avenue
Springfield 65802
417-895-7130

St. Louis Community College
at Florissant Valley
3400 Pershall Road
St. Louis 63135-1499
314-595-4250

St. Louis Community College
at Forest Park
5600 Oakland Avenue
St. Louis 63110-1316
314-644-9131

East Central Missouri Junior College
P.O. Box 529
Union 63084-0529
314-583-5195

Central Missouri State University
School of Public Service
Warrensburg 64093
816-543-4290

MONTANA
Montana State University
College of Technology-Great Falls
2100 16th Avenue South
Great Falls 59405
406-771-4312

Helena College of Technology
of the University of Montana
Helena 59601
406-444-6800

Miles Community College
Miles City 59301-4799
406-233-3513

NEBRASKA
Southeast Community College
Lincoln Campus
8800 "O" Street
Lincoln 68520-1299
402-437-2604

University of Nebraska-Lincoln
14th & R Streets
Lincoln 68588-0417
402-472-2030

Mid-Plains Technical Community
College
Interstate 20 and Highway 83
North Platte 69101-9491
308-532-8740

University of Nebraska at Omaha
College of Engineering
P.O. Box 688
Omaha 68182
402-554-2709

NEVADA
Western Nevada Community College
2201 West Nye Lane
Carson City 89701
702-887-3038

Northern Nevada Community College
901 Elm Street
Elko 89801-3348
702-738-8493

Clark County Community College
3200 East Cheyenne Avenue
Las Vegas 89030
702-643-6060

Community College of Southern
Nevada
Cheyenne Campus
3200 East Cheyenne Avenue
North Las Vegas 89030-4296
702-651-4060

Truckee Meadows Community College
7000 Dandini Blvd.
Reno 89512-3901
702-673-7042

NEW HAMPSHIRE
New Hampshire Vocational Technical
College
Route 106 Prescott Hill
Laconia 03246
603-524-3207

NEW JERSEY
Camden County College
P.O. Box 200
Blackwood 08012-0200
609-227-7200

Union County College
1033 Springfield Avenue
Cranford 07016-1528
908-709-7500

Middlesex County College
155 Mill Road
Edison 08818-3050
732-906-2510

Jersey City State College
2039 Kennedy Blvd.
Jersey City 07305
201-200-2000

Brookdale Community College
Newman Springs Road
Lincroft 07738-1599
908-224-2262

Essex County College
303 University Avenue
Newark 07102-1798
973-877-3119

Sussex Community College
College Hills
Newton 07860
201-579-5400

Passaic County Community College
One College Blvd.
Patterson 07505-1179
973-684-6304

Burlington County College
Pemberton 08068-1599
609-894-9311

Union County Vocational Technical
Institute
1776 Raritan Road
Scotch Plains 07076
908-889-8288

Ocean County College
College Drive
Toms River 08754-2001
732-255-0304

Mercer County Community College
1200 Old Trenton Road
Trenton 08690-1004
609-586-4800

Thomas Edison State College
101 West State Street
Trenton 08608-1176
609-292-6565

Essex County College, Westchester
Campus
730 Bloomfield Avenue
West Caldwell 07006
201-228-3968

NEW MEXICO
New Mexico State University at
Alamogordo
P.O. Box 477
North Scenic Drive
Alamogordo 88310
505-437-6860

Albuquerque Technical Vocational
Institute
525 Buena Vista Southeast
Albuquerque 87106-4096
505-224-3210

New Mexico State University-Carlsbad
1500 University Drive
Carlsbad 88220-3509
505-887-7533

Clovis Community College
417 Schepps Blvd.
Clovis 88101
505-769-4025

New Mexico Junior College
5317 Lovington Highway
Hobbs 88240-9123
505-392-5092

Dona Ana Branch Community College
Box 30001, Dept. 3DA
Las Cruces 88003-8001
505-527-7532

Eastern New Mexico University-Roswell
Roswell 88202-6000
505-624-7149

NEW YORK
Cayuga County Community College
197 Franklin Street
Auburn 13021-3099
315-255-1743

Broome Community College
Upper Front Street
P.O. Box 1017
Binghamton 13902-1017
607-778-5000

Corning Community College
One Academic Drive
Corning 14830-3297
607-962-9221

Mercy College
555 Broadway
Dobbs Ferry 10522
914-674-7324

John Jay College of Criminal Justice
City University of New York
445 West 59th Street
New York 10019
212-237-8000

Erie Community College-South Campus
4041 Southwestern Blvd.
Orchard Park 14127-2199
716-851-1003

Monroe Community College
1000 East Henrietta Road
P.O. Box 9720
Rochester 14623-5780
716-292-2000

Schenectady County Community
College
78 Washington Avenue
Schenectady 12305-2294
518-381-1366

Rockland Community College
145 College Road
Suffern 10901-3699
914-574-4237

Onondaga Community College
4941 Onondaga Hill Road
Syracuse 13215
315-469-2201

NORTH CAROLINA

Central Piedmont Community College
P.O. Box 35009
Charlotte 28235-5009
704-330-6464

Gaston College
201 Highway 321 South
Dallas 28834
704-922-6214

Durham Technical Community College
1637 Lawson Street
Durham 27703-5023
919-686-3629

Alamance Community College
P.O. Box 8000
Graham 27253
910-578-2002

Coastal Carolina Community College
444 Western Blvd.
Jacksonville 28546-6877
910-455-1221

Guilford Technical Community College
P.O. Box 309
Jamestown 27282-0309
910-334-4822, ext. 5350

Lenoir Community College
P.O. Box 188
Kinston 28502-0188
919-527-6223

Davidson County Community College
P.O. Box 1287
Lexington 27293-1287
910-249-8186

Cape Fear Community College
411 North Front Street
Wilmington 28401
910-251-5100

Wilson Technical Community College
P.O. Box 4305
Wilson 27893-3310
919-291-1195

OHIO

University of Akron
381 East Bukchtel Common
Akron 44325-2001
330-972-6428

Bowling Green State University
Continuing Education Division
504 Administration Building
Bowling Green 43402
419-372-2531

Stark Technical College
6200 Frank Avenue NW
Canton 44720-7299
330-966-5450

University of Cincinnati
College of Applied Science
100 East Central Park
Cincinnati 45216
513-556-1100

Cuyahoga Community College
Metropolitan Campus
2900 Community College Avenue
Cleveland 44115
216-987-4030

Columbus Technical Institute
550 Spring Street
Columbus 43216-1609
614-227-2669

Sinclair Community College
444 West 3rd Street
Dayton 45402-1460
513-226-3000

Delaware Junior Vocational School
1610 State Route 521
Delaware 43015-9001
614-363-1993

Lorain County Community College
1005 Abbe Road North
Elyria 44035
216-365-4191

Lakeland Community College
7700 Clocktower Drive
Kirtland 44094
216-953-7106

Hocking Technical College
3301 Hocking Parkway
Nelsonville 45764-9588
614-753-3591

Stark Technical College
6200 Frank Avenue
North Canton 44720
330-966-5450

Cuyahoga Community College
Western Campus
11000 Pleasant Valley Road
Parma 44130-5199
216-987-5154

Owens Community College-Toledo
P.O. 10000
Oregon Road
Toledo 43699-1947
419-661-7225

OKLAHOMA
University of Oklahoma
407 West Boyd
Norman 73019
405-325-2151

Oklahoma State University
Technical Institute
900 North Portland Street
Oklahoma City 73107-6120
405-945-3270

Oklahoma State University
301 Campus Fire Station
Stillwater 74078
405-744-5358

Tulsa Junior College
909 South Boston Avenue
Tulsa 74119
918-595-7000

OREGON
Clatsop Community College
1653 Jerome Avenue
Astoria 97103-3698
503-325-0910

Central Oregon College
2600 Northwest College Way
Bend 97701-5998
541-383-7500

Southwestern Oregon Community
College
1988 Newmark
Coos Bay 97420-2912
541-888-7339

Lane Community College
4000 East 30th Avenue
Eugene 97405
541-741-3072

Rogue Community College
3345 Redwood Highway
Grants Pass 97527-9298
541-471-3500

Mt. Hood Community College
2600 SE Stark
Gresham 97030-3300
503-667-7368

Eastern Oregon State College
1410 "L" Avenue
La Grande 97850
503-962-3393

Western Oregon State College
345 North Monmouth Avenue
Monmouth 97361
503-838-8211

Portland Community College
1200 SW 49th Avenue
Portland 97280-0990
503-414-2227

Umpqua Community College
P.O. Box 967
Roseburg 97470-0226
541-440-4616

Chemeketa Community College
4000 Lancaster Drive NE
Salem 97309-7070
503-399-5006

PENNSYLVANIA
Westmoreland County Community
College
Armbrust Road 15697
412-925-4077

Montgomery County Community
College
340 Dekalb Pike
Blue Bell 19422-0796
215-641-6550

Butler County Area Vocational Tech
School
210 Campus Lane
Butler 16001
412-282-0735

Harrisburg Area Community College
1 HACC Drive
Harrisburg 17110-2999
717-780-2406

Delaware County Community College
Media 19063-1094
610-359-5333

Community College of Allegheny
County
Boyce Campus
595 Beatty Road
Monroeville 15146
412-327-1327

Luzerne County Community College
Prospect Street & College Middle Road
Nanticoke 18634-9804
717-740-7336

Community College of Philadelphia
1700 Spring Garden Street
Philadelphia 19130-3991
215-751-8000

Community College of Allegheny
County
South Campus
1750 Clairton Road
West Mifflin 15122
412-469-6300

Westmoreland County Community
College
Armbrust Road
Youngwood 15697
412-925-1150

RHODE ISLAND
Providence College
School of Continuing Education
Providence 02918
401-865-2535

Community College of Rhode Island
400 East Avenue
Warwick 02886-1807
401-825-2285

SOUTH CAROLINA
Beaufort Technical College
P.O. Box 1288
100 South Ribout Road
Beaufort 29902
803-525-8313

Greenville Technical College
P.O. Box 5616
Greenville 29606-5616
803-250-8603

Midlands Technical College
Airport Campus
1260 Lexington Drive
West Columbia 29170
803-738-1400

SOUTH DAKOTA
Kilian Community College
224 North Phillips Avenue
Sioux Falls 57104-6014
605-336-1711

TENNESSEE
Chattanooga State Technical
Community College
4501 Amnicola Highway
Chattanooga 37406-1018
423-697-4400

Tennessee Tech Center at Crump
P.O. Box 89, Hwy 64 West
Crump 38327
901-632-3393

Volunteer State Community College
1480 Nashville Pike
Gallatin 37066-3188
615-452-8600

Roane State Community College
Patton Lane
Harriman 37748
615-354-3000

Memphis State University
University College
Memphis 38152
901-678-2716

State Technical Institute at Memphis
598? Macon Cove
Memphis 38134-7693
901-383-4195

Tennessee Technology Center
at Murfreesboro
1303 Old Fort Parkway
Murfreesboro 37130
615-898-8010

TEXAS
Cisco Junior College
841 North Judge Ely Blvd.
Abilene 79601-4624
915-673-4567

Texas Engineering Extension Service
Regional Training Center
3650 Loop 322
Abilene 79602
409-845-7225

Amarillo Community College
P.O. Box 447
Amarillo 79178-0001
806-371-5030

Trinity Valley Community College
500 South Prairieville
Athens 75751
903-675-6357

Austin Community College
1212 Rio Grand
Austin 78701
512-223-3030

Beaumont Institute
P.O. Box 10043
Beaumont 77710
409-880-8185

Texas Southmost College
80 Fort Brown Street
Brownsville 78520-4991
210-544-8254

Blinn College, Bryan Campus
1909 South Texas Avenue
Bryan 77802
409-821-0220

Conroe Area Vocational School
3200 West Davis
Conroe 77304
409-760-6659

Del Mar College
101 Baldwin
Corpus Christi 78404-3897
512-886-1255

Navarro College
3200 West 7th Avenue
Corsicano 75110
903-874-6501

El Centro College
Main and Lamar Streets
Dallas 75202-3604
214-860-2311

El Paso Community College
6601 Dyer Street
P.O. Box 20500
El Paso 79998-0500
915-594-2150

Fort Worth Fire Training Academy
1000 Calvert
Fort Worth 76107
817-871-6875

Tarrant County Junior College
1500 Houston Street
Fort Worth 76102-6599
817-515-7851

Galveston College
4015 Avenue "Q"
Galveston 77550-7496
409-763-6551

Hill College of the Hill
Junior College District
112 Lamar Drive
Hillsboro 76645-0619
817-582-2555

Houston Community College
4310 Dunlaby
Houston 77006
713-718-5000

Kilgore College
100 Broadway
Kilgore 75662
903-984-8531

Laredo Community College
West End Washington Street
Laredo 78040
210-721-5108

South Plains College
1302 Main Street
Lubbock 79401
806-894-9611

Collin County Community College
2200 West University Drive
McKinney 75069
214-548-6710

Midland College
3600 North Garfield
Midland 79705-6399
915-685-4500

Odessa College
201 West University
Odessa 79764-7127
915-335-6575

San Jacinto College
Central Campus
8060 Spencer Highway
Pasadena 77501-2007
281-476-1819

San Antonio College
1300 San Pedro Avenue
San Antonio 78212-4299
210-733-2581

Tyler Junior College
P.O. Box 9020
Tyler 75711-9020
903-510-2523

UTAH
Utah Valley State College
800 West 1200 South
Oren 84058-0001
801-222-8461

VERMONT
Southeastern Vermont Career Education
Center
Fairground Road
Brattleboro 05301
802-257-7335

VIRGINIA
Northern Virginia Community College
8333 Little River Turnpike
Annandale 22003-3796
703-323-3000

Thomas Nelson Community College
P.O. Box 9407
Hampton 23670-0407
757-825-2800

J. Sargeant Reynolds Community
College
108 East Grace Street
P.O. Box 85622
Richmond 23285-5622
804-371-3029

Tidewater Community College
Virginia Beach Campus
1700 College Crescent
Virginia Beach 23456
804-427-7100

WASHINGTON
Bellevue Community College
3000 Landerholm Circle, S.E.
Bellevue 98007-6484
206-641-2222

Olympic College
Bremerton 98337-1699
360-478-4542

Lower Columbia College
Longview 98632-0310
360-577-2304

Edmonds Community College
20000 68th Ave "W"
Lynnwood 98036-5999
206-640-1416

South Puget Sound Community College
Olympia 98512-6292
360-754-7711

Columbia Basin Community College
2600 North 20th Avenue
Pasco 99301-3397
509-547-0511

Spokane Community College
North 1810 Greene Street
Spokane 99207-5399
509-533-7015

Bates Vocational Technical Institute
1101 South Yakima Avenue
Tacoma 98405-4895
206-964-6591

Fort Steilacoom Community College
9401 Farwest Drive SW
Tacoma 99498
206-964-6591

Wenatchee Valley College
1300 Fifth Street
Wenatchee 98801-1799
509-664-2563

Yakima Valley Community College
S. 16th Avenue at Nob Hill Blvd.
P.O. Box 1647
Yakima 98907-1647
509-574-4713

WEST VIRGINIA
Shepherd College
Shepherdstown 25443-3210
304-876-5212

WISCONSIN
Fox Valley Technical College
1825 North Bluemond Road
P.O. Box 888
Appleton 54913-2277
414-735-5645

Lakeshore Technical Institute
1290 North Street
Cleveland 53015
414-458-4183

Chippewa Valley Technical College
620 West Clairemont Avenue
Eau Claire 54701-6120
715-833-6246

Moraine Park Technical College
235 North National Avenue
Fond du Lac 54935
414-922-8611

Northeast Wisconsin Technical College
2740 West Mason Street
Green Bay 53407-9042
414-498-5400

Blackhawk Technical College
2228 Center Avenue
Janesville 53547-5009
608-757-7713

Madison Area Technical College
211 North Carroll Street
Madison 53704
608-258-2300

Milwaukee Area Technical College
700 West State Street
Milwaukee 53233-1443
414-297-6301

Wisconsin Indianhead Technical College
1019 South Knowles Avenue
New Richmond 54017
715-246-6561

Milwaukee Area Technical College
South Campus
6665 South Howell Avenue
Oak Creek 53154
414-571-4500

Gateway Technical College
1001 South Main Street
Racine 53403
414-656-7350

Mid-State Technical College
500 32nd Street North
Wisconsin Rapids 54494
715-422-5319

WYOMING
Casper College
125 College Drive
Casper 82601-4699
307-268-2491

Laramie County Community College
1400 East College Drive
Cheyenne 82007-3299
307-778-5222

Participating Colleges/ Universities: Open Learning Fire Service Program
Cogswell College
10420 Bubb Road
Cupertino, CA 95014
408-252-5550
Contact: Linda Fladger
States served: AZ, CA, NV

University of Cincinnati
College of Applied Science
2220 Victory Parkway
Cincinnati, OH 45206
513-556-6583
Contact: Barbara Barkley
States served: FL, GA, IN, MI, MN, ND, OH, SD, WI

Memphis State University
University College
Johnson Hall, G-1
Memphis, TN 38152
901-678-2716
Contact: Dr. Susanne Darnell
States served: AL, AR, KY, LA, MS, TN, SC

Western Oregon State College
Division of Continuing Education
Monmouth, OR 97361
503-838-8483
Contact: Cynthia Wilcox or Dori Beeks
States served: AK, CO, HI, ID, MT, OR, UT, WA, WY

University of Maryland/
University College
Open Learning Program
University Blvd., at Adelphi Road
College Park, MD 20742
301-985-7722
Toll-free in MD: 800-888-UMUC
Toll-free in VA: 800-866-3726
Contact: JoAnne Hildebrand
States served: DE, MD, NJ, NC, DC, WV, VA

Western Illinois University
Educational Broadcasting and
Independent Study
305 Memorial Hall
Macomb, IL 61455
309-298-2182
Contact: Dr. Joyce Nielsen
States served: IL, IA, KS, MO, NE, NM, OK, TX

State University of New York (SUNY)
Empire State College
Center for Distance Learning
2 Union Avenue
Saratoga Springs, NY 12866
518-587-2100, ext. 300
Contact: Fire Service Coordinator
States served: CT, ME, MA, NH, NY, PA, RI, VT

THE INSIDE TRACK

Who:	Kevin Scarbrough
What:	Fire Inspector
Where:	Ann Arbor Fire Department, Ann Arbor, Michigan
How long:	Twelve years in Ann Arbor Fire Department; 20 years total in the Fire Service

Insider's Advice:

It's a very competitive field, so you need to get as much training and practical experience as possible. In Ann Arbor, we only hire about 10-15 people a year from a pool of around 600 applicants. When I give lectures to teenagers who are interested in becoming firefighters, I tell them to make sure they keep a squeaky clean record, so they will have a chance to get their application looked at. If you have speeding tickets, or any police record in your background and your application is next to ten others that don't have anything negative on their records, who do you think is going to get picked?

Also, put in as many applications and cards of interest as you can to all the fire departments around you. You may be able to request a transfer to the fire department you really want to work for once you get in. The hardest part is getting in, so don't be too selective about where you apply. It's also good to get experience as a volunteer firefighter or in an ambulance service to get some hands-on practical experience.

Insider's Take on the Future:

I am very happy in my job as a fire inspector, although I could always go back into fire suppression if I wanted to.

CHAPTER | 4

This chapter covers how to receive financial aid for the training program you want to attend. You'll find out how to determine your eligibility for financial aid, how to distinguish among the different types of aid, how to gather your financial records, and how to file your forms once you have completed them. A sample financial aid form is included.

FINANCIAL AID FOR THE TRAINING YOU NEED

Now that you have decided that landing a job in fire protection services is what you really want to do, and you have chosen a training program, you need a plan for financing your training. That is what this chapter is all about. You can qualify for aid at several different types of schools, ranging from community colleges, technical colleges, universities, and vocational schools that offer short-term training programs, certificates, associate degrees, and bachelor's degrees. You can often qualify for some type of financial aid even if you're attending only part time. The financial aid you'll get may be less than in full-time programs, but it can still be worthwhile and help you pay for a portion of your fire services training program.

Don't let financial aid anxiety deter you from finding out more about the many options you have for financing your training program. Take a deep breath, relax, and plunge into this chapter knowing that you can get a handle on the whole financial aid process during the time it takes you to finish this chapter. There are additional books you can read that are devoted to financial aid, some of which are listed at the end of this chapter. Also, most schools have good financial aid advisors, who can address your concerns and help you fill out the necessary paperwork. So there is no shortage of information available to help you. Take advantage of it today!

SOME MYTHS ABOUT FINANCIAL AID

There's a lot of confusion out there about financial aid. Here are three of the most common myths that need to be cleared up before digging into the financial aid process.

Myth #1: All the red tape involved in finding sources and applying for financial aid is too confusing for me.

Fact: It's really not as confusing as people say it is. The whole financial aid process is a set of steps that are ordered and logical. Besides, several sources of help are available to you. For instance, reading this chapter will give you a helpful overview of the entire process and give you tips on how to get the most financial aid you can. There are also resources at the end of this chapter that you can go to for additional help. If you believe you'll be able to cope with college, you'll surely be able to cope with looking for the money to go, especially if you take the process one step at a time in an organized manner.

Myth #2: For most students financial aid just means getting a loan and going into heavy debt, which isn't worth it, or working while in school, which will lead to burn-out and poor grades.

Fact: In addition to federal grants and scholarships, most schools have their own grants and scholarships, which the student doesn't have to pay back, and many students get these; it's also possible to get a combination of scholarships and loans. It's worth taking out a loan if it means attending the school you really want to attend, rather than settling for second choice or not going to school at all. As for working while in school, it's true that it is a challenge to hold down a full-time or even part-time job while in school, but a small amount of work-study employment while attending classes (10-12 hours per week) actually improves academic performance because it teaches students important time-management skills.

Myth #3: I can't understand the financial aid process because of all the unfamiliar terms and strange acronyms that are used.

Fact: While you will encounter an amazing number of acronyms and some unfamiliar terms while applying for federal financial aid, you can refer to the handy acronym list and glossary at the end of this chapter for quick definitions and clear explanations of the commonly used terms and acronyms.

GETTING STARTED

The first step in beginning the financial aid process is to get a form that is called *Free Application for Federal Student Aid* (FAFSA). You can get this form from several sources: your public library, your school's financial aid office, on-line at http://www.finaid.org/finaid.html, or by calling 1-800-4-FED-AID. You need to get an original form to mail in, however; photocopies of federal forms are not acceptable. In financial aid circles, this form is commonly referred to by its initials: FAFSA. The FAFSA determines your eligibility status for all grants and loans provided by federal or state governments and certain college or institutional aid; therefore, it is the first step in the financial aid process, and it should be done as soon as possible.

Many sources of financial aid require students to complete a FAFSA in order to become eligible for other types of financial aid, such as school-based or private aid. If you are computer savvy, you can visit a Web site where you fill out and submit the FAFSA on-line. You'll need to print out, sign, and send in the release and signature pages. See the *Resources* section at the end of this chapter for the web address.

The second step of the process is to create a financial aid calendar. You can use any standard calendar—wall, desk, or portable—for this step. The main thing is to write all of the application deadlines for each step of the financial aid process on one calendar, so you can see at a glance what needs to be done when. You can start this calendar by writing in the date you requested your FAFSA. Then mark down when you received it and when you sent the completed form in. Add important dates and deadlines for any other applications you need to complete for school-based or private aid as you progress though the financial aid process. Using and maintaining a calendar will help the whole financial aid process run more smoothly and give you peace of mind that the important dates are written down and are not merely bouncing around in your head.

Determining Your Eligibility

To receive federal financial aid from an accredited college or institution's student aid program, you must:

- have a high school diploma or a General Education Development (GED) certificate, pass a test approved by the U. S. Department of Education, or meet other standards your state establishes that are approved by the U. S. Department of Education
- be enrolled or accepted for enrollment as a regular student working toward a degree or certificate in an eligible program
- be a U. S. citizen or eligible non-citizen possessing a social security number. Refer to Immigration and Naturalization Service (INS) in the section entitled *Financial Aid Resources* that appears at the end of this chapter if you are not a U.S. citizen and are unsure of your eligibility.
- have a valid social security number
- make satisfactory academic progress
- sign a statement of educational purpose and a certification statement on overpayment and default
- register with selective services, if required
- have financial need, except for some loan and other aid programs

You are eligible to apply for federal financial aid by completing the FAFSA even if you haven't yet been accepted or enrolled in a school. However, you do need to be enrolled in an accredited training program in order to actually receive any funds from a federal financial aid program.

When to Apply

Apply for financial aid as soon as possible after January 1st of the year in which you want to enroll in school. For example, if you want to begin school in the fall of 1998, then you should apply for financial aid as soon as possible after January 1, 1998. It is easier to complete the FAFSA after you have completed your tax return, so you may want to consider filing your taxes as early as possible as well. *Do not sign, date, or send your application before January 1st of the year for which you are seeking aid.* If you apply by mail, send your completed application in the envelope that came with the original application. The envelope is already addressed, and using it will make sure your application reaches the correct address.

Many students lose out on thousands of dollars in grants and loans because they file too late. A financial aid administrator from New Jersey says:

> When you fill out the Free Application for Federal Student Aid (FAFSA), you are applying for all aid available, both federal and state,

work-study, student loans, etc. The important thing is complying with the deadline date. Those students who do are considered for the Pell Grant, the SEOG (Supplemental Educational Opportunity Grant), and the Perkins Loan, which is the best loan as far as interest goes. Lots of students miss the June 30th deadline, and it can mean losing $2,480 from TAG, about $350 from WPCNJ, and another $1,100 from EOF. Students, usually the ones who need the money most, often ignore the deadlines.

After you mail in your completed FAFSA, your application will be processed in approximately four weeks. Then, you will receive a Student Aid Report (SAR) in the mail. The SAR will report the information from your application and, if there are no questions or problems with your application, your SAR will report your Expected Family Contribution (EFC), the number used to determine your eligibility for federal student aid. Each school you list on the application may also receive your application information if the school is set up to receive the information electronically.

You must reapply for financial aid every year. However, after your first year, you will receive a Student Aid Report (SAR) in the mail before the application deadline. If no corrections need to be made, you can just sign it and send it in.

Getting Your Forms Filed

Getting your forms filed is as simple as one, two, three.

1. Get an original Federal Application for Federal Student Aid (FAFSA).

Remember to pick up an original copy of this form as photocopies are not acceptable.

2. Fill out the entire FAFSA as completely as possible.

Make an appointment with a financial aid counselor if you need help. Read the forms completely, and don't skip any relevant portions.

3. Return the FAFSA before the deadline date.

Financial aid counselors warn that many students don't file the forms before the deadline and lose out on available aid. Don't be one of those students!

Financial Need

Financial aid from many of the programs discussed in this chapter is awarded on the basis of financial need (except for unsubsidized Stafford, PLUS, and Consolidation loans, and some scholarships and grants). When you apply for federal student aid by completing the FAFSA, the information you report is used in a formula established by the U. S. Congress. The formula determines your Expected Family Contribution (EFC), an amount you and your family are expected to contribute toward your education. If your EFC is below a certain amount, you'll be eligible for a federal Pell grant, assuming you meet all other eligibility requirements.

There isn't a maximum EFC that defines eligibility for the other financial aid options. Instead, your EFC is used in an equation to determine your financial needs.

> **Cost of Attendance – EFC = Financial Need**

A financial aid administrator calculates your cost of attendance and subtracts the amount you and your family are expected to contribute toward that cost. If there's anything left over, you're considered to have financial need.

Are You Considered Dependent or Independent?

You need to find out if you are considered to be a dependent or an independent student by the federal government. Federal policy uses strict and specific criteria to make this designation, and that criteria applies to all applicants for federal student aid equally. A dependent student is expected to have parental contribution to school expenses, and an independent student is not. The parental contribution depends on the number of parents with earned income, their income and assets, the age of the older parent, the family size, and the number of family members enrolled in post-secondary education. Income is not just the adjusted gross income from the tax return, but also includes nontaxable income such as social security benefits and child support.

You're an independent student if at least one of the following applies to you:

* you were born before January 1, 1974
* you're married (even if you're separated)
* you have legal dependents other than a spouse who get more than half of their support from you and will continue to get that support during the award year
* you're an orphan or ward of the court (or were a ward of the court until age 18)
* you're a graduate or professional student

- you're a veteran of the U. S. Armed Forces—formerly engaged in active service in the US Army, Navy, Air Force, Marines, or Coast Guard or as a cadet or midshipman at one of the service academies—released under a condition other than dishonorable. (ROTC students, members of the National Guard, and most reservists are not considered veterans, nor are cadets and midshipmen still enrolled in one of the military service academies.)

If you live with your parents and if they claimed you as a dependent on their last tax return then your need will be based on your parents' income. You do not qualify for independent status just because your parents have decided to not claim you as an exemption on their tax return (this used to be the case but is no longer) or do not want to provide financial support for your college education.

Students are classified as dependent or independent because federal student aid programs are based on the idea that students (and their parents or spouse, if applicable) have the primary responsibility for paying for their post-secondary, i.e., after high school, education.

Gathering Financial Records

Your financial need for most grants and loans depends on your financial situation. Now that you've determined if you are considered a dependent or independent student, you'll know whose financial records you need to gather for this step of the process. If you are a dependent student, then you must gather not only your own financial records, but also those of your parents because you must report their income and assets as well as your own when you complete the FAFSA. If you are an independent student, then you need to gather only your own financial records (and those of your spouse if you're married). Gather your tax records from the year previous to when you are applying. For example, if you apply for the fall of 1998, you will use your tax records from 1997.

To help you fill out the FAFSA, gather the following documents:

- U. S. Income Tax Returns (IRS Form 1040, 1040A, or 1040EZ) for the year that just ended and W-2 and 1099 forms
- Records of untaxed income, such as Social Security benefits, AFDC or ADC, child support, welfare, pensions, military subsistence allowances, and veterans benefits
- Current bank statements and mortgage information

- Medical and dental expenses for the past year that weren't covered by health insurance
- Business and/or farm records
- Records of investments such as stocks, bonds, and mutual funds, as well as bank Certificates of Deposit (CDs) and recent statements from money market accounts
- Social Security number(s)

Even if you do not complete your federal income tax return until March or April, you should not wait to file your FAFSA until your tax returns are filed with the IRS. Instead, use estimated income information and submit the FAFSA, as noted earlier, just as soon as possible after January 1. Be as accurate as possible, but you can correct estimates later.

TYPES OF FINANCIAL AID

There are many types of financial aid available to help with school expenses. Three general categories exist for financial aid:

1. Grants and scholarships—aid that you don't have to pay back
2. Work/Study—aid that you earn by working
3. Loans—aid that you have to pay back

Grants

Grants are an advantageous form of financial aid because they do not need to be paid back. They are normally awarded based on financial need. Here are the two most common forms of grants:

Federal Pell Grants

Federal Pell grants are based on financial need and are awarded only to undergraduate students who have not yet earned a bachelor's or professional degree. For many students, Pell grants provide a foundation of financial aid to which other aid may be added. Awards for the award year will depend on program funding. The maximum award for the 1996-1997 award year was $2,470. You can receive only one Pell grant in an award year, and you may not receive Pell grant funds for more than one school at a time.

How much you get will depend not only on your Expected Family Contribution (EFC) but also on your cost of attendance, whether you're a full-time or part-time student, and whether you attend school for a full academic year or less. You can qualify for a Pell grant even if you are only enrolled part time in a training program. You should also be aware that some private and school-based sources of financial aid will not consider your eligibility if you haven't first applied for a Pell grant.

Federal Supplemental Educational Opportunity Grants (FSEOG)

A Federal Supplemental Educational Opportunity Grant (FSEOG) is for undergraduates with exceptional financial need—that is, students with the lowest Expected Family Contributions (EFCs). It gives priority to students who receive federal Pell grants. An FSEOG is similar to a Pell grant in that it doesn't need to be paid back.

You can receive between $100 and $4,000 a year, depending on when you apply, your level of need, and the funding level of the school you're attending. There's no guarantee that every eligible student will be able to receive a FSEOG. Students at each school are paid based on the availability of funds at that school and not all schools participate in this program. To have the best chances of getting this grant, apply as early as you can after January 1st of the year in which you plan to attend school.

Scholarships

Scholarships are almost always awarded for academic merit or for special characteristics (for example, ethnic heritage, interests, sports, parents' career, college major, geographic location) rather than financial need. The best aspect of scholarships is that you don't have to pay them back! You can obtain scholarships from federal, state, school, and private sources.

To find private sources of aid, spend a few hours in the library looking at scholarship and fellowship books or consider a reasonably priced (under $30) scholarship search service. See the *Resources* section at the end of this chapter to find contact information for search services and scholarship book titles. Another place to check is in fire service magazines. If you're currently employed, check to see if your employer has aid funds available. If you're a dependent student, ask your parents, aunts, uncles, and cousins to check with groups or organizations they belong to for possible aid sources. You never know what type of private aid you might dig up. For example, any of the following groups may know of money that could be yours:

- religious organizations
- fraternal organizations
- clubs, such as the Rotary, Kiwanas, American Legion, or 4H
- athletic clubs
- veterans groups
- ethnic group associations
- unions

If you have already selected the school you will attend, check with a financial aid administrator (FAA) in the financial aid department to find out if you qualify for any school-based scholarships or other aid. More schools are offering merit-based aid for students with a high school GPA of a certain level or with a certain level of SAT scores in order to attract more students to their school. Also check with the Fire Science department to see if they maintain a bulletin board or other method of posting available scholarships that are specific to fire science programs.

While you are looking for sources of scholarships, continue to enhance your chances of winning a scholarship by participating in extracurricular events and volunteer activities. You should also obtain references from people who know you well and are leaders in the community, so you can submit their names and/or letters with your scholarship applications. Make a list of any awards you've received in the past or other honors that you could list on your scholarship application.

Here are a few samples of scholarships that you might be eligible for.

National Merit Scholarships
About 5,000 students each year receive this scholarship, based solely on academic performance in high school, from the National Merit Scholarship Corporation. If you are a high school senior who has excellent grades and who has scored high on tests such as the ACT and SAT, this scholarship may be for you.

Hope Scholarship
The Hope Scholarship is a Georgia lottery funded scholarship for students who keep a 3.0 Grade Point Average or higher.

New Hampshire Charitable Fund Student Aid Program
The New Hampshire Charitable Fund Student Aid Program offers scholarships to New Hampshire residents.

Military Scholarships

Military scholarships such as the G.I. Bill are available if you are applying to the Army, Navy, Air Force, or Marines, and you may get other money for college or to pay off previous loans.

Yvorra Leadership Development Foundation

The Yvorra Leadership Development Foundation offers scholarships to members of emergency service organizations. These include volunteer, part-paid, and career personnel from fire departments, rescue squads, and emergency medical services. Contact them at P.O. Box 408, Port Republic, MD 20676 or at 410-586-3048 for more information.

International Association of Arson Investigators (IAAI)

The IAAI offers scholarships of $1,000 for undergraduate students enrolled in fire science programs at two- and four-year institutions. Must be a member of IAAI or sponsored by a member. Write to The John Charles Wilson Scholarship Fund at 300 S. Broadway, Suite #100, St. Louis, MO 63102.

Maryland State Higher Education Commission

Maryland residents who are pursuing a degree in firefighting, or other safety majors at a Maryland school who agree to serve in Maryland as firefighters or rescue squad members for a certain amount of time after graduation, may be eligible for a scholarship from the Maryland State Higher Education Commission. The scholarship awards reimbursement of firefighting training up to a maximum of $2,620. Contact Maryland State Higher Education Commission, 16 Francis Street, Annapolis, MD 21401 for more information.

Texas Higher Education Coordinating Board

Applicants must be firefighters enrolled in a fire science degree program. The scholarship award is an exemption from tuition at public colleges or universities in Texas. Contact the Texas Higher Education Coordinating Board, P.O. Box 12788, Austin, TX 78711 for more information.

For a complete list of contact information for every state's higher education department, see Appendix A under *Higher Education Departments*.

Work-Study Programs

A variety of work-study programs exist for students. If you already know what school you want to attend, you can find out about its school-based work-study options from the student employment office. Job possibilities may include on- or off-campus jobs, part time or almost full time, in the fire or EMT field or in an unrelated area. Another type of work study program is called the Federal Work-Study program, and it can be applied for on the FAFSA.

The Federal Work-Study (FWS) program provides jobs for undergraduate and graduate students *with financial need,* allowing them to earn money to help pay education expenses. The program encourages community service work and provides hands-on experience related to your course of study, when available. The amount of the FWS award depends on:

* when you apply (again, *apply early*)
* your level of need
* the funds available at your particular school

Your FSW salary will be at least the current federal minimum wage or higher, depending on the type of work you do and the skills required. As an undergraduate, you'll be paid by the hour (a graduate student may receive a salary), and you will receive the money directly from your school at least monthly—you cannot be paid by commission or fee. The awards are not transferable from year to year. Not all schools have work-study programs in every area of study.

An advantage of working under the FWS program is that your earnings are exempt from FICA taxes if you are enrolled full time and are working less than half time. You will be assigned a job on-campus, in a private non-profit organization, or a public agency that offers a public service. You may provide a community service relating to fire or other emergency service if your school has such a program. Some schools have agreements with private for-profit companies, if the work demands your fire or other emergency skills. The total hourly wages you earn in each year cannot exceed your total FWS award for that year and you cannot work more than twenty hours per week. Your financial aid administrator (FAA) or the direct employer must consider your class schedule and your academic progress before assigning your job.

If you cannot finance your entire training program through scholarships, grants, or work-study exclusively, the next step is to consider taking out a loan. Be cautious about the amount you borrow, but remember that it may be worth it to borrow money to attend a training program that will enhance your future job prospects.

Student Loans

The first step in finding a student loan is to know the basics of loan programs. You need to become familiar with the student loan programs, especially with government loans. You can get a good head start on this process by reading the rest of this chapter. To get more detailed information than appears here, seek guidance from a financial aid administrator or banking institution.

Questions to Ask Before You Take out a Loan

In order to get the facts and clearly understand the loan you're about to take out, ask the following questions:

1. *What is the interest rate and how often is the interest capitalized?* Your college's financial aid administrator (FAA) may be able to tell you this.
2. *What fees will be charged?* Government loans generally have an origination fee that goes to the federal government to help offset its costs, and a guarantee fee, which goes to a guaranty agency for insuring the loan. Both are deducted from the amount given to you.
3. *Will I have to make any payments while still in school?* Usually you won't, and, depending on the type of loan, the government may even pay the interest for you while you're in school.
4. *What is the grace period—the period after my schooling ends, during which no payment is required?* Is the grace period long enough, realistically, for you to find a job and get on your feet? (A six-month grace period is common.)
5. *When will my first payment be due and approximately how much will it be?* You can get a good preview of the repayment process from the answer to this question.
6. *Who exactly will hold my loan? To whom will I be sending payments? Who should I contact with questions or inform of changes in my situation?* Your loan may be sold by the original lender to a secondary market institution. You need to know the contact information for your lender, however.
7. *Will I have the right to pre-pay the loan, without penalty, at any time?* Some loan programs allow pre-payment with no penalty but others do not.

8. *Will deferments and forbearances be possible if I am temporarily unable to make payments?* You need to find out how to apply for a deferment or forbearance if you need it.
9. *Will the loan be canceled ("forgiven") if I become totally and permanently disabled, or if I die?* This is always a good option to have on any loan you take out.

Federal Perkins Loans

A federal Perkins loan has the lowest interest (currently, it's 5%) of any loan available for both undergraduate and graduate students and is offered to students with exceptional financial need. You repay your school, who lends the money to you with government funds.

Depending on when you apply, your level of need, and the funding level of the school, you can borrow up to $3,000 for each year of undergraduate study. The total amount you can borrow as an undergraduate is $15,000.

The school pays you directly by check or credits your tuition account. You have nine months after you graduate (provided you were continuously enrolled at least half-time) to begin repayment, with up to 10 years to pay off the entire loan.

PLUS Loans (Loans for Parents)

PLUS loans enable parents with good credit histories to borrow money to pay education expenses of a child who is a dependent undergraduate student enrolled at least half time. Your parents must submit the completed forms to your school.

To be eligible, your parents will be required to pass a credit check. If they don't pass the credit check, they might still be able to receive a loan if they can show that extenuating circumstances exist or if someone who is able to pass the credit check agrees to co-sign the loan. Your parents must also meet citizenship requirements.

The yearly limit on a PLUS Loan is equal to your cost of attendance minus any other financial aid you receive. For instance, if your cost of attendance is $6,000 and you receive $4,000 in other financial aid, your parents could borrow up to, but no more than, $2,000. The interest rate varies, but is not to exceed 9% over the life of the loan. Your parents must begin repayment while you're still in school. There is no grace period.

Federal Stafford Loans

Federal Stafford loans are low-interest loans that are given to students who attend school at least half time. The lender of the loans is usually a bank or credit union;

however, sometimes a school may be the lender. Stafford loans are either subsidized or unsubsidized.

- **Subsidized loans** are awarded on the basis of financial need. You will not be charged any interest before you begin repayment or during authorized periods of deferment. The federal government "subsidizes" the interest during these periods.
- **Unsubsidized loans** are not awarded on the basis of financial need. You'll be charged interest from the time the loan is disbursed until it is paid in full. If you allow the interest to accumulate, it will be capitalized—that is, the interest will be added to the principal amount of your loan, and additional interest will be based upon the higher amount. This will increase the amount you have to repay.

If you're a dependent undergraduate student, you can borrow up to:

- $2,625 if you're a first-year student enrolled in a program that is at least a full academic year.
- $3,500 if you've completed your first year of study and the remainder of your program is at least a full academic year.
- $5,500 a year if you've completed two years of study and the remainder of your program is at least a full academic year.

If you're an independent undergraduate student or a dependent student whose parents are unable to get a PLUS Loan, you can borrow up to:

- $6,625 if you're a first-year student enrolled in a program that is at least a full academic year.
- $7,500 if you've completed your first year of study and the remainder of your program is at least a full academic year.

There are many borrowing limit categories to these loans, depending on whether you get an unsubsidized or subsidized loan, which year in school you're enrolled, how long your program of study is, and if you're independent or dependent. You can have both kinds of Stafford loans at the same time, but the total amount of money loaned at any given time cannot exceed $23,000. The interest rate varies, but should not exceed 8.25%. An origination fee for a Stafford loan is approximately 3 or 4 percent of the loan, and the fee will be deducted from each loan disbursement you receive. There is a six-month grace period after graduation before you must start repaying the loan.

Federal Direct Student Loans

You should be aware of federal direct student loans, which are a part of a relatively new program. The loans have basically the same terms as the federal Stafford student loans and the PLUS loans for parents. The main difference is that the U. S. Department of Education is the lender instead of a bank. One advantage to federal direct student loans is that they offer a variety of repayment terms, such as a fixed monthly payment for ten years or a variable monthly payment for up to twenty-five years that is based on a percentage of income. Be aware that not all colleges participate in this loan program.

General Guidelines for all Types of Loans

Before you commit yourself to any loans, be sure to keep in mind that these are loans, not grants or scholarships, so plan ahead and make sure that you don't borrow more than you'll be able to repay. Estimate realistically how much you'll earn when you leave school and remember that you'll have other monthly obligations such as housing, food, and transportation expenses.

Once you're in school

Once you have your loan (or loans) and you're attending classes, don't forget about the responsibility of your loan. Keep a file of information on your loan that includes copies of all your loan documents and related correspondence, along with a record of all your payments. Open and read all your mail about your education loan.

Remember also that you are obligated by law to notify both your Financial Aid Administrator (FAA) and the holder or servicer of your loan if there is a change in your:

- name
- address
- enrollment status (dropping to less than half-time means that you'll have to begin payment six months later)
- anticipated graduation date

After you leave school

After you leave school you must either begin repaying your student loan, or you may get a grace period. For example, if you have a Stafford loan you will be provided with a six-month grace period before your first payment is due; other types of loans have grace periods as well. And, if you haven't been out in the world of work before, with your loan repayment you'll begin your credit history. If you make payments on time, you'll build up a good credit rating, and credit will be easier for you to obtain for other things. Get off to a good start, so you don't run the risk of going into default. If you default (or refuse to pay back your loan) any number of the following things could happen to you as a result:

+ have trouble getting any kind of credit in the future
+ no longer qualify for federal or state educational financial aid
+ have holds placed on your college records
+ have your wages garnished
+ have future federal income tax refunds taken
+ have your assets seized

To avoid the negative consequences of going into default in your loan, be sure to do the following:

+ Open and read all mail you receive about your education loans immediately.
+ Make scheduled payments on time. Since interest is calculated daily, delays can be costly.
+ Contact your servicer immediately if you can't make payments on time. Your servicer may be able to get you into a graduated or income-sensitive/ income contingent repayment plan or work with you to arrange a deferment or forbearance. In spite of the horror stories you might hear, loan officials can be quite helpful if you don't try to evade your responsibility.

There are very few circumstances under which you won't have to repay your loan. If you become permanently and totally disabled, you probably will not have to (providing the disability did not exist prior to your obtaining the aid). Likewise if you die, if your school closes permanently in the middle of the term, or if you are erroneously certified for aid by the financial aid office. However, if you're simply disappointed in your program of study or don't get the job you wanted after graduation, you are not relieved of your obligation.

Remember, too, that there are restrictions on how you can use your loan money. It's to be used strictly for education-related expenses (for example, tuition, fees, books, room and board, transportation, and so on). A CD of your favorite rock band now and then won't hurt, or if you really need a toaster oven you can get by with that. But don't use your loan to buy expensive clothing, fund elaborate vacations, or buy a new car.

Loan Repayment

When it comes time to repay your loan, you will make payments to your original lender, to a secondary market institution to which your lender has sold your loan, or to a loan servicing specialist acting as its agent to collect payments. At the beginning of the process, try to choose the lender who offers you the best benefits (for example, a lender who lets you pay electronically, offers lower interest rates to those who consistently pay on time, or who has a toll-free number to call 24 hours a day, 7 days a week). Ask the financial aid administrator at your college to direct you to such lenders.

Be sure to check out your repayment options before borrowing. Lenders are required to offer repayment plans that will make it easier to pay back your loans. Your repayment options may include:

- Standard repayment: full principal and interest payments due each month throughout your loan term. You'll pay the least amount of interest using the standard repayment plan, but your monthly payments may seem high when you're just out of school.
- Graduated repayment: interest-only or partial interest monthly payments due early in repayment. Payment amounts increase thereafter. Some lenders offer interest-only or partial interest repayment options which provide the lowest initial monthly payments available.
- Income-based repayment: monthly payments are based on a percentage of your monthly income.
- Consolidation loan: allows the borrower to consolidate several types of federal student loans with various repayment schedules into one loan. This loan is designed to help student or parent borrowers simplify their loan repayments. The interest rate on a consolidation loan may be lower than what you're currently paying on one or more of your loans. The phone number for loan consolidation at the William D. Ford Direct Loan Program is 800-557-7392. Financial administrators recommend that you

do not consolidate a Perkins loan with any other loans since the interest on a Perkins loan is already the lowest available. Loan consolidation is not available from all lenders.

- Prepayment: paying more than is required on your loan each month or in a lump sum is allowed for all federally-sponsored loans at any time during the life of the loan without penalty. Prepayment will reduce the total cost of your loan.

It's quite possible—in fact likely—that while you're still in school your FFELP loan will be sold to a secondary market institution such as Sallie Mae. You'll be notified of the sale by letter, and you need not worry if this happens—your loan terms and conditions will remain exactly the same or they may even improve. Indeed, the sale may give you repayment options and benefits that you would not have had otherwise. Your payments after you finish school, and your requests for information should be directed to the new loan holder.

If you receive any interest-bearing student loans, you will have to attend exit counseling after graduation, where the loan lenders will tell you the total amount of debt and work out a payment schedule with you to determine the amount and dates of repayment. Many loans do not become due until at least six to nine months after you graduate, giving you a grace period. For example, you do not have to begin paying on the Perkins loan until nine months after you graduate. This grace period is to give you time to find a good job and start earning money. However, during this time, you may have to pay the interest on your loan.

If for some reason you remain unemployed when your payments become due, you may receive an unemployment deferment for a certain length of time. For many loans, you will have a maximum repayment period of 10 years (excluding periods of deferment and forbearance).

THE MOST FREQUENTLY ASKED QUESTIONS ABOUT FINANCIAL AID

Here are answers to the most frequently asked questions about student financial aid:

1. *I probably don't qualify for aid—should I apply for it anyway?* Yes. Many students and families mistakenly think they don't qualify for aid and fail to apply. Remember that there are some sources of aid that are not based on need. The FAFSA form is free—there's no good reason for not applying.

2. *Do I need to be admitted at a particular university before I can apply for financial aid?* No. You can apply for financial aid any time after January 1. However, to get the funds, you must be admitted and enrolled in school.

3. *Do I have to reapply for financial aid every year?* Yes, and if your financial circumstances change, you may get either more or less aid. After your first year you will receive a "Renewal Application" which contains preprinted information from the previous year's FAFSA. Renewal of your aid also depends on your making satisfactory progress toward a degree and achieving a minimum GPA.

4. *Are my parents responsible for my educational loans?* No. You and you alone are responsible, unless they endorse or co-sign your loan. Parents are, however, responsible for the federal PLUS loans. If your parents (or grandparents or uncle or distant cousins) want to help pay off your loan, you can have your billing statements sent to their address.

5. *If I take a leave of absence from school, do I have to start repaying my loans?* Not immediately, but you will after the grace period. Generally, though, if you use your grace period up during your leave, you'll have to begin repayment immediately after graduation, *unless* you apply for an extension of the grace period *before* it's used up.

6. *If I get assistance from another source, should I report it to the student financial aid office?* Yes, definitely—and, sadly, your aid amount will probably be lowered accordingly. But you'll get into trouble later on if you don't report it.

7. *Where can I get information about federal student financial aid?* Call 1-800-4-FED-AID (1-800-433-3243) or 1-800-730-8913 (if hearing impaired) and ask for a free copy of *The Student Guide: Financial Aid from the U.S. Department of Education.* You can also write to the Federal Student Aid Information Center, PO Box 84, Washington, DC 20044.

8. *Are federal work-study earnings taxable?* Yes, you must pay federal and state income tax, although you may be exempt from FICA taxes if you are enrolled full time and work less than 20 hours a week.

9. *Where can I obtain a copy of the FAFSA?* Your guidance counselor should have the forms available. You can also get the FAFSA from the financial aid office at a local college, your local public library, or by calling 1-800-4-FED-AID.

10. *Are photocopies of the FAFSA acceptable?* No. Only the original FAFSA form produced by the U.S. Department of Education is acceptable. Photocopies, reproductions, and faxes are not acceptable.

11. *My parents are separated or divorced. Which parent is responsible for filling out the FAFSA?* If your parents are separated or divorced, the custodial parent is responsible for filling out the FAFSA. The custodial parent is the parent with whom you lived the most during the past 12 months. Note that this is not necessarily the same as the parent who has legal custody. The question of which parent must fill out the FAFSA becomes complicated in many situations, so you should take your particular circumstance to the student financial aid office for help.

Financial Aid Checklist

____ Explore your options as soon as possible after you've decided to begin a training program.

____ Find out what your school requires and what financial aid they offer.

____ Complete and mail the FAFSA as soon as possible after January 1st.

____ Complete and mail other applications by the deadlines.

____ Gather loan application information and forms from your college financial aid office.

____ Forward the certified loan application to a participating lender: bank, savings and loan institution, or credit union, if necessary.

____ Carefully read all letters and notices from the school, the federal student aid processor, the need analysis service, and private scholarship organizations. Note whether financial aid will be sent before or after you are notified about admission, and how exactly you will receive the money.

____ Report any changes in your financial resources or expenses to your financial aid office so they can adjust your award accordingly.

____ Re-apply each year.

Financial Aid Acronyms Key	
COA	Cost of Attendance
CWS	College Work-Study
EFC	Expected Family Contribution
EFT	Electronic Funds Transfer
ESAR	Electronic Student Aid Report
ETS	Educational Testing Service
FAA	Financial Aid Administrator
FAF	Financial Aid Form
FAFSA	Free Application for Federal Student Aid
FAO	Financial Aid Office
FDSLP	Federal Direct Student Loan Program
FFELP	Federal Family Education Loan Program
FSEOG	Federal Supplemental Educational Opportunity Grant
FWS	Federal Work-Study
GSL	Guaranteed Student Loan
PC	Parent Contribution
PLUS	Parent Loan for Undergraduate Students
SAP	Satisfactory Academic Progress
SC	Student Contribution
SLS	Supplemental Loan for Students

FINANCIAL AID TERMS—CLEARLY DEFINED

Accrued interest: Interest that accumulates on the unpaid principal balance of your loan.

Capitalization of interest: Addition of accrued interest to the principal balance of your loan which increases both your total debt and monthly payments.

Default (you won't need this one, right?)**:** Failure to repay your education loan.

Deferment: A period when a borrower, who meets certain criteria, may suspend loan payments.

Delinquency (you won't need this one, either!)**:** Failure to make payments when due.

Disbursement: Loan funds issued by the lender.

Forbearance: Temporary adjustment to repayment schedule for cases of financial hardship.

Grace period: Specified period of time after you graduate or leave school during which you need not make payments.

Holder: The institution that currently owns your loan.

In-school grace, and deferment interest subsidy: Interest the federal government pays for borrowers on some loans while the borrower is in school, during authorized deferments, and during grace periods.

Interest: Cost you pay to borrow money.

Interest-only payment: A payment that covers only interest owed on the loan and none of the principal balance.

Lender (Originator): Puts up the money when you take out a loan. Most lenders are financial institutions, but some state agencies and schools make loans too.

Origination fee: Fee, deducted from the principal, that is paid to the federal government to offset its cost of the subsidy to borrowers under certain loan programs.

Principal: Amount you borrow, which may increase as a result of capitalization of interest, and the amount on which you pay interest.

Promissory note: Contract between you and the lender that includes all the terms and conditions under which you promise to repay your loan.

Secondary markets: Institutions that buy student loans from originating lenders, thus providing lenders with funds to make new loans.

Servicer: Organization that administers and collects your loan. May be either the holder of your loan or an agent acting on behalf of the holder.

Subsidized Stafford loans: Loans based on financial need. The government pays the interest on a subsidized Stafford loan for borrowers while they are in-school and during specified deferment periods.

Unsubsidized Stafford loans: Loans available to borrowers, regardless of family income. Unsubsidized Stafford loan borrowers are responsible for the interest during in-school, deferment periods, and repayment.

FINANCIAL AID RESOURCES

Here are several additional resources that you can use to obtain more information about financial aid.

Telephone Numbers

These phone numbers may be of help to you when completing your financial aid application forms:

Federal Student Aid Information Center (U. S. Department of Education)
Hotline...800-4-FED-AID (800-433-3243)
TDD Number for Hearing-Impaired...800-730-8913
For suspicion of fraud or abuse of federal aid 800-MIS-USED (800-647-8733)
Selective Service..847-688-6888
Immigration and Naturalization (INS) 415-705-4205
Internal Revenue Service (IRS) 800-829-1040
Social Security Administration...800-772-1213
National Merit Scholarship Corporation 708-866-5100
Sallie Mae's College AnswerSM Service.......................................800-222-7183
Career College Association 202-336-6828
ACT: American College Testing program...................................916-361-0656
(about forms submitted to the need analysis servicer)
College Scholarship Service (CSS) ....609-771-7725; TDD 609-883-7051
Need Access/Need Analysis Service...800-282-1550
FAFSA on the WEB Processing/Software Problems............................800-801-0576

Internet Web Sites

Check out these Web sites for information about financial aid:
www.ed.gov/prog_info/SFAStudentGuide.
The *Student Guide* is a free informative brochure about financial aid and is available on-line at the Department of Education's Web address listed here.

http://www.ed.gov\prog_info\SFA\FAFSA
This site offers students help in completing the FAFSA.

http://www.ed.gov/offices/OPE/t4_codes.html.
This site offers a list of Title IV school codes that you may need to complete the FAFSA.

http://www.ed.gov/offices/OPE/express.html

This site enables you to fill out and submit the FAFSA on-line. You'll need to print out, sign, and send in the release and signature pages.

www.finaid.org/finaid

This is one of the most comprehensive Web sites for financial aid information. They have many pages addressing special situations, such as international students, bankruptcy, defaulting on student loans, divorced parents, financially unsupportive parents, and myths about financial aid.

http://www.finaid.org/finaid/phone.html

This site lists telephone numbers specific to loan programs, loan consolidations, tuition payment plans, and state prepaid tuition plans.

http://www.finaid.org/finaid/documents.html

Free on-line documents can be found at this site.

http://www.finaid.org/finaid/vendors/software.html

Software for EFC calculators and financial aid planning and advice are at this site.

www.career.org

This is the Web site of the Career College Association (CCA). It offers a limited number of scholarships for attendance at private proprietary schools. Contact CCA for further information at 750 First Street, NE, Suite 900, Washington, DC 20002-4242 or visit their Web site.

www.salliemae.com

Web site for Sallie Mae that contains information about loan programs.

http://www.fastweb.com

This site is called FastWEB. If you answer a few simple questions for them (such as name and address, geographical location, associations and organizations that you are affiliated with, age, and so on), they will give you a free list of possible scholarships you might qualify for. Their database is updated regularly, and your list gets updated when new scholarships are added that fit your profile. FastWEB boasts that more than 20,000 students access their site every day.

Scholarship Search Services

If you find financial aid information overwhelming, or if you simply don't have the time to do the footwork yourself, you may want to hire a scholarship search service. Be aware that a reasonable price is $30-$50. If the service wants to charge more, investigate it carefully. Scholarship search services usually only provide you with a list of six or so sources of scholarships that you then need to check out and apply for.

Software Programs

Cash for Class
800-205-9581
FAX: 714-673-9039

Redheads Software, Inc.
3334 East Coast Highway #216
Corona del Mar, CA 92625
E-mail: cashclass@aol.com

C-LECT Financial Aid Module
800-622-7284 or 315-497-0330
FAX: 315-497-3359
Chronicle Guidance Publications
P.O. Box 1190
Moravia, NY 13118-1190

Peterson's Award Search
800-338-3282 or 609-243-9111
Peterson's
P.O. Box 2123
Princeton, NJ 08543-2123
E-mail: custsvc@petersons.com

Pinnacle Peak Solutions (Scholarships 101)

800-762-7101 or 602-951-9377

FAX: 602-948-7603

Pinnacle Peak Solutions

7735 East Windrose Drive

Scottsdale, AZ 85260

TP Software—Student Financial Aid Search Software

800-791-7791 or 619-496-8673

TP Software

P.O. Box 532

Bonita, CA 91908-0532

E-mail: mail@tpsoftware.com

Books and Pamphlets

Take a look at any of the following books and pamphlets to get more information about the financial aid process.

The Student Guide

Published by the U.S. Department of Education, this is *the* handbook about federal aid programs. To get a printed copy, call 1-800-4-FED-AID.

Looking for Student Aid

Published by the U.S. Department of Education, this is an overview of sources of information about financial aid. To get a printed copy, call 1-800-4-FED-AID.

How Can I Receive Financial Aid for College?

Published from the Parent Brochures ACCESS ERIC Web site. Order a printed copy by calling 800-LET-ERIC or write to ACCESS ERIC, Research Blvd-MS 5F, Rockville, MD 20850-3172.

The Best Resources for College Financial Aid 1996/97, by Michael Osborn.

Published by Resource Pathways Inc., 1996. This book lists resources available to students, parents, and counselors—books, Web sites, CD-ROMs, videos, software—and then recommends the most useful for each stage in the financial aid and scholarship search. It includes a concise description and evaluation of each resource.

10-Minute Guide to Paying for College by William D. Van Dusen and Bart Astor. Published by Arco Publishing, 1996. A quick, simple, step-by-step guide for getting through the financial aid process that answers the most pressing financial aid questions. Both parents and students will appreciate this easy-to-use book.

College Financial Aid for Dummies, by Herm Davis and Joyce Kennedy. Published by IDG Books Worldwide, 1997. This fun and friendly reference guides readers through the financial aid maze by covering the major types of loans, grants, and scholarships available with strategies for how to find and secure them.

Other Related Financial Aid Books:

Annual Register of Grant Support. Chicago: Marquis, Annual.

A's and B's of Academic Scholarships. Alexandria, VA: Octameron, Annual.

Chronicle Student Aid Annual. Moravia, NY: Chronicle Guidance, Annual.

College Blue Book: Scholarships, Fellowships, Grants and Loans. New York: Macmillan, Annual.

College Financial Aid Annual. New York: Arco, Annual.

Directory of Financial Aid for Minorities. San Carlos, CA: Reference Service Press, Biennial.

Directory of Financial Aid for Women. San Carlos, CA: Reference Service Press, Biennial

Don't Miss Out: the Ambitious Student's Guide to Financial Aid. Robert and Ann Leider. Alexandria, VA: Octameron, Annual.

Financial Aid for Higher Education. Dubuque: Wm. C. Brown, Biennial.

Financial Aid for the Disabled and their Families. San Carlos, CA: Reference Service Press, Biennial.

Paying Less for College. Princeton: Peterson's Guides, Annual.

Free Application for Federal Student Aid
1997–98 School Year

WARNING: If you purposely give false or misleading information on this form, you may be fined $10,000, sent to prison, or both.

"You" and "your" on this form always mean the student who wants aid.

Form Approved
OMB No. 1840-0110
App. Exp. 6/30/98

U.S. Department of Education
Student Financial
Assistance Programs

Use dark ink. Make capital letters and numbers clear and legible. | E X M 2 4 | *Fill in ovals completely.* Only one oval per question. ● Correct | *Incorrect marks will be ignored.* Incorrect ⊗ ☑

Section A: You (the student)

1–3. Your name

1. Last name 2. First name 3. M.I.

Your title (optional) Mr. ○ 1 Miss, Mrs., or Ms. ○ 2

4–7. Your permanent mailing address
(All mail will be sent to this address. See Instructions, page 2 for state/country abbreviations.)

4. Number and street (Include apt. no.)

5. City 6. State 7. ZIP code

8. Your social security number (SSN) *(Don't leave blank. See Instructions, page 2.)*

9. Your date of birth Month Day Year 1 9

10. Your permanent home telephone number Area code

11. Your state of legal residence State

12. Date you became a legal resident of the state in question 11 *(See Instructions, page 2.)* Month Day Year 1 9

13–14. Your driver's license number *(Include the state abbreviation. If you don't have a license, write in "None.")*
State License number

15–16. Are you a U.S. citizen?
(See Instructions, pages 2–3.)
Yes, I am a U.S. citizen. ○ 1
No, but I am an eligible noncitizen. ○ 2
A [   ]
No, neither of the above. ○ 3

17. As of today, are you married? *(Fill in only one oval.)*
I am not married. (I am single, widowed, or divorced.) ○ 1
I am married. ○ 2
I am separated from my spouse. ○ 3

18. Date you were married, separated, divorced, or widowed. If divorced, use date of divorce or separation, whichever is earlier.
(If never married, leave blank.) Month Year 1 9

19. Will you have your first bachelor's degree before July 1, 1997? Yes ○ 1 No ○ 2

Section B: Education Background

20–21. Date that you (the student) received, or will receive, your high school diploma, either—
(Enter one date. Leave blank if the question does not apply to you.)
- by graduating from high school **20.** Month Year 1 9
OR
- by earning a GED **21.** Month Year 1 9

22–23. Highest educational level or grade level your father and your mother completed. *(Fill in one oval for each parent. See Instructions, page 3.)*

	22. Father	23. Mother
elementary school (K–8)	○ 1	○ 1
high school (9–12)	○ 2	○ 2
college or beyond	○ 3	○ 3
unknown	○ 4	○ 4

If you (and your family) have **unusual circumstances**, complete this form and then check with your financial aid administrator. Examples:
- tuition expenses at an elementary or secondary school,
- unusual medical or dental expenses not covered by insurance,
- a family member who recently became unemployed, or
- other unusual circumstances such as changes in income or assets that might affect your eligibility for student financial aid.

Section C: Your Plans *Answer these questions about your college plans.*

Page 2

24–28. Your expected enrollment status for the 1997–98 school year
(See Instructions, page 3.)

School term	Full time	3/4 time	1/2 time	Less than 1/2 time	Not enrolled
24. Summer term '97	○ 1	○ 2	○ 3	○ 4	○ 5
25. Fall semester/qtr. '97	○ 1	○ 2	○ 3	○ 4	○ 5
26. Winter quarter '97-98	○ 1	○ 2	○ 3	○ 4	○ 5
27. Spring semester/qtr. '98	○ 1	○ 2	○ 3	○ 4	○ 5
28. Summer term '98	○ 1	○ 2	○ 3	○ 4	○ 5

29. Your course of study *(See Instructions for code, page 3.)*

Code

30. College degree/certificate you expect to receive *(See Instructions for code, page 3.)*

31. Date you expect to receive your degree/certificate

Month   Day   Year

32. Your grade level during the 1997–98 school year *(Fill in only one.)*

- 1st yr./never attended college ○ 1
- 1st yr./attended college before ○ 2
- 2nd year/sophomore ○ 3
- 3rd year/junior ○ 4
- 4th year/senior ○ 5
- 5th year/other undergraduate ○ 6
- 1st year graduate/professional ○ 7
- 2nd year graduate/professional ○ 8
- 3rd year graduate/professional ○ 9
- Beyond 3rd year graduate/professional ○ 10

33–35. In addition to grants, what other types of financial aid are you (and your parents) interested in? *(See Instructions, page 3.)*

33. Student employment   Yes ○ 1   No ○ 2

34. Student loans   Yes ○ 1   No ○ 2

35. Parent loans for students   Yes ○ 1   No ○ 2

36. If you are (or were) in college, do you plan to attend **that same college** in 1997–98? *(If this doesn't apply to you, leave blank.)*   Yes ○ 1   No ○ 2

37. For how many dependents will you (the student) pay child care or elder care expenses in 1997–98?

38–39. Veterans education benefits you expect to receive from July 1, 1997 through June 30, 1998

38. Amount per month $ _____.00

39. Number of months

Section D: Student Status

40. Were you born **before** January 1, 1974? .... Yes ○ 1   No ○ 2

41. Are you a veteran of the U.S. Armed Forces? .... Yes ○ 1   No ○ 2

42. Will you be enrolled in a graduate or professional program (beyond a bachelor's degree) in 1997-98? ...... Yes ○ 1   No ○ 2

43. Are you married? .... Yes ○ 1   No ○ 2

44. Are you an orphan or a ward of the court, or **were** you a ward of the court until age 18? .... Yes ○ 1   No ○ 2

45. Do you have legal dependents (**other than a spouse**) that fit the definition in Instructions, page 4? .... Yes ○ 1   No ○ 2

If you answered "**Yes**" to **any** question in Section D, go to Section E and fill out **both the GRAY and the WHITE** areas on the rest of this form.

If you answered "**No**" to **every** question in Section D, go to Section E and fill out **both the GREEN and the WHITE** areas on the rest of this form.

Section E: Household Information

Remember:
At least one "Yes" answer in Section D means fill out the GRAY and WHITE areas.

All "No" answers in Section D means fill out the GREEN and WHITE areas.

STUDENT (& SPOUSE)

46. Number in your household in 1997–98
(Include yourself and your spouse. Do not include your children and other people unless they meet the definition in Instructions, page 4.)

47. Number of college students in household in 1997–98
(Of the number in 46, how many will be in college at least half-time in at least one term in an eligible program? Include yourself. See Instructions, page 4.)

PARENT(S)

48. Your parent(s)' **current** marital status:

- single ○ 1
- married ○ 2
- separated ○ 3
- divorced ○ 4
- widowed ○ 5

State

49. Your parent(s)' state of legal residence

50. Date your parent(s) became legal resident(s) of the state in question 49 *(See Instructions, page 5.)*

Month   Day   Year
1 9

51. Number in your parent(s)' household in 1997–98
(Include yourself and your parents. Do not include your parents' other children and other people unless they meet the definition in Instructions, page 5.)

52. Number of college students in household in 1997–98
(Of the number in 51, how many will be in college at least half-time in at least one term in an eligible program? Include yourself. See Instructions, page 5.)

Section F: 1996 Income, Earnings, and Benefits *You must see Instructions, pages 5 and 6, for information about tax forms and tax filing status, especially if you are estimating taxes or filing electronically or by telephone. These instructions will tell you what income and benefits should be reported in this section.* Page 3

The following 1996 U.S. income tax figures are from:

	STUDENT (& SPOUSE) *Everyone must fill out this column.* 53. *(Fill in one oval.)*	PARENT(S) 65. *(Fill in one oval.)*
A—a completed 1996 IRS Form 1040A, 1040EZ, or 1040TEL	○ 1	A ○ 1
B—a completed 1996 IRS Form 1040	○ 2	B ○ 2
C—an estimated 1996 IRS Form 1040A, 1040EZ, or 1040TEL	○ 3	C ○ 3
D—an estimated 1996 IRS Form 1040	○ 4	D ○ 4
E—will not file a 1996 U.S. income tax return	*(Skip to question 57.)* ○ 5	E *(Skip to 69.)* ○ 5

1996 Total number of exemptions (Form 1040–line 6d, or 1040A–line 6d; 1040EZ filers— *see Instructions, page 6.*) **54.** **66.**

TAX FILERS ONLY

1996 Adjusted Gross Income (AGI: Form 1040–line 31, 1040A–line 16, or 1040EZ–line 4 *see Instructions, page 6.*) **55.** $ .00 **67.** $ .00

1996 U.S. income tax **paid** (Form 1040–line 44, 1040A–line 25, or 1040EZ–line 10) **56.** $ .00 **68.** $ .00

1996 Income earned from work (Student) **57.** $ .00 (Father) **69.** $ .00

1996 Income earned from work (Spouse) **58.** $ .00 (Mother) **70.** $ .00

1996 Untaxed income and benefits (yearly totals only):

Earned Income Credit (Form 1040–line 54, Form 1040A–line 29c, or Form 1040EZ–line 8) **59.** $ .00 **71.** $ .00

Untaxed Social Security Benefits **60.** $ .00 **72.** $ .00

Aid to Families with Dependent Children (AFDC/ADC) **61.** $ .00 **73.** $ .00

Child support received for all children **62.** $ .00 **74.** $ .00

Other untaxed income and benefits from Worksheet #2, page 11 **63.** $ .00 **75.** $ .00

1996 Amount from Line 5, Worksheet #3, page 12 *(See Instructions.)* **64.** $ .00 **76.** $ .00

Section G: Asset Information   ATTENTION!

Fill out Worksheet A or Worksheet B in Instructions, page 7. *If you meet the tax filing and income conditions on Worksheets A and B, you do not have to complete Section G to apply for Federal student aid. Some states and colleges, however, require Section G information for their own aid programs. Check with your financial aid administrator and/or State Agency.*

Age of your older parent **84.**

	STUDENT (& SPOUSE)	PARENT(S)
Cash, savings, and checking accounts	**77.** $ .00	**85.** $ .00
Other real estate and investments value *(Don't include the home.)*	**78.** $ .00	**86.** $ .00
Other real estate and investments debt *(Don't include the home.)*	**79.** $ .00	**87.** $ .00
Business value	**80.** $ .00	**88.** $ .00
Business debt	**81.** $ .00	**89.** $ .00
Investment farm value *(See Instructions, page 8.)* *(Don't include a family farm.)*	**82.** $ .00	**90.** $ .00
Investment farm debt *(See Instructions, page 8.)* *(Don't include a family farm.)*	**83.** $ .00	**91.** $ .00

SAMPLE

Section H: Releases and Signatures

92–103. What college(s) do you plan to attend in 1997–98?
(Note: The colleges you list below will have access to your application information. See Instructions, page 8.)

Housing codes	1—on-campus	3—with parent(s)
	2—off-campus	4—with relative(s) other than parent(s)

	Title IV School Code	College Name	College Street Address and City	State	Housing Code
XX.	0 5 4 3 2 1	EXAMPLE UNIVERSITY	14930 NORTH SOMEWHERE BLVD. ANYWHERE CITY	S T	XX. 2
92.					93.
94.					95.
96.					97.
98.					99.
100.					101.
102.					103.

104. The U.S. Department of Education will send information from this form to your state financial aid agency and the state agencies of the colleges listed above so they can consider you for state aid. Answer **"No"** if you **don't** want information released to the state. *(See Instructions, page 9 and "Deadlines for State Student Aid," page 10.)* ....104. No ○ 2

105. Males not yet registered for Selective Service (SS): Do you want SS to register you? *(See Instructions, page 9.)* ....105. Yes ○ 1

106–107. Read, Sign, and Date Below

All of the information provided by me or any other person on this form is true and complete to the best of my knowledge. I understand that this application is being filed jointly by all signatories. If asked by an authorized official, I agree to give proof of the information that I have given on this form. I realize that this proof may include a copy of my U.S. or state income tax return. I also realize that if I do not give proof when asked, the student may be denied aid.

Statement of Educational Purpose. I certify that I will use any Federal Title IV, HEA funds I receive during the award year covered by this application solely for expenses related to my attendance at the institution of higher education that determined or certified my eligibility for those funds.

Certification Statement on Overpayments and Defaults. I understand that I may not receive any Federal Title IV, HEA funds if I owe an overpayment on any Title IV educational grant or loan or am in default on a Title IV educational loan unless I have made satisfactory arrangements to repay or otherwise resolve the overpayment or default. I also understand that I must notify my school if I do owe an overpayment or am in default.

Everyone whose information is given on this form should sign below. The student (and at least one parent, if parental information is given) must sign below or this form will be returned unprocessed.

106. Signatures *(Sign in the boxes below.)*

1 Student

2 Student's Spouse

3 Father/Stepfather

4 Mother/Stepmother

107. Date completed | Month | Day | Year | 1997 ○ | 1998 ○

Section I: Preparer's Use Only

For preparers other than student, spouse, and parent(s). Student, spouse, and parent(s), sign in question 106.

Preparer's name (last, first, MI)

Firm name

Firm or preparer's address (street, city, state, ZIP)

108. Employer identification number (EIN)

OR

109. Preparer's social security number

Certification: All of the information on this form is true and complete to the best of my knowledge.

110. Preparer's signature | **Date**

School Use Only

D/O ○ | Title IV Code

FAA Signature

MDE Use Only
Do not write in this box | Special handle

MAKE SURE THAT YOU HAVE COMPLETED, DATED, AND SIGNED THIS APPLICATION.
Mail the original application (NOT A PHOTOCOPY) to: Federal Student Aid Programs, P.O. Box 4008, Mt. Vernon, IL 62864-8608

THE INSIDE TRACK

Who:	Timo Rova
What:	Smoke Jumper
Where:	Works out of Montana; fights fires all over the U.S.
How long:	Four years as a smoke jumper; nine years as a firefighter

Insider's Advice:

It's usually easier to get a firefighting job on the state level first, and then you can apply on the federal level after you get some experience. My main advice is be proactive and apply to as many agencies as possible and don't give up when you're looking for your first job. Call each forest and ask for the Fire Management Officer (FMO) to find out how and when they'll be hiring. There's usually an open season in February or March when they accept applications. Then keep calling to find out more information, and each time you call ask if they'd mind if you call again to check on your status. You know the saying: *the squeaky wheel gets the grease*, so make lots of calls. You also have to be willing to move around, and realize that it takes time to get in. Once you get in somewhere, it will take awhile to move up the ranks.

Some people become firefighters and want to become smoke jumpers right away, but you really need to gain experience first. It usually takes, at the very least, five or six years to build up to becoming a smoke jumper. You have to start by becoming a basic firefighter, then you can move up to working in an engine company, and then becoming a "hot shot," which is a type-one team that fights on the fire's front lines. The top rung of the firefighting ladder is the smoke-jumper position. It's a tough job, but you can prepare for it by getting in excellent physical shape. The recruit training camp for smoke jumpers is brutal; half of my class didn't make it through. I barely made it—it was very physically demanding work.

Insider's Take on the Future:

I would like to put my fire experience to use in a management role, either as a Fire Management Officer (FMO) or as a Trainer on the federal level. I'm already training new firefighters on the state level, so I know that I enjoy that type of work. I really love being a smoke jumper, but I know I can't keep it up forever. It's really tough on the body to do for a long time. Plus, I really enjoy working with people and teaching, so a management career in firefighting would be a good next step for me.

CHAPTER | 5

This chapter shows how you can best succeed once you've landed your job as a firefighter. You'll find out what qualities are rewarded and how to move up the ranks. Advancement opportunities and other fire-related career options are clearly explained.

HOW TO SUCCEED ON THE JOB

You can achieve success in your firefighting career in many different ways. When you talk to firefighters, you'll find that most of them enjoy their job, so chances are that you will too once you get your feet wet. While the job may seem overwhelming when you first start out, you'll get adjusted soon enough. Before long, you may even seek to take on additional responsibilities and training.

STEPPING STONES TO SUCCESS

There are many avenues to pursue as a firefighter. First of all, you need to succeed in your job as a probationary firefighter before you can be fully admitted and sworn in as an official firefighter in good standing. After that, the paths open up to include a wealth of advancement options, from attaining Firefighter II certification, to becoming a lieutenant or captain, all the way to eventually landing a job as a fire chief. Several other fire-related career paths are open to you as well, from fire code enforcement officer to arson investigator and more. Read on to find out how you can succeed as a firefighter and to see what exciting future career possibilities are available in the fire service field.

Succeeding as a Probationary Firefighter

After you get hired by a fire department, you'll most likely be automatically enrolled in a fire training course that will give you the specific information you need to know in that particular fire department. In large urban fire departments, new recruits are normally trained for several weeks at the department's training center. Smaller fire departments may send you to a state or county fire academy. Either way, the training you receive as a newly hired firefighter is often considered the "boot camp" for new firefighters. The physical demands are rigorous and may include a variety of tasks, such as using axes, saws, chemical extinguishers, ladders, and other equipment during simulated emergencies. Classroom work is also usually required of new firefighters. Of course, the training of new firefighters differs from state to state because some states require job applicants to obtain Firefighter I certification before they can even apply for a job and other states won't allow you to get certified as a firefighter until after you are hired. Regardless of the amount and intensity of the training you receive as a newly hired firefighter, it will be a challenge to learn the standard operating procedures (SOP) of the particular fire department for which you are working.

Fitting into the Fire House Culture

Since newly hired firefighters must undergo a period of probation—ranging from 6 to 18 months, depending on the department's requirements—they need to be extremely vigilant. During the probation period, either you or the company you work for may decide that you aren't cut out to be a firefighter, so it's important to do your best, apply yourself, foster a teamwork attitude, and follow orders during your probationary period. You may have heard horror stories of how *probies* are treated (*probies* is the term that is commonly used in the firefighting world to refer to new firefighters who are on probationary status). Don't be alarmed if you find that you are suddenly the brunt of all the practical jokes or if senior firefighters constantly ask you for favors or taunt you. In many fire departments, it's just the routine practice of "breaking in the probies" as some senior firefighters like to call it. The best way to deal with this type of treatment is to quickly develop a strong sense of humor toward it, unless, of course, it becomes unbearable or dangerous. You've heard the saying "grin and bear it." You don't want to make enemies, get a reputation as a stick in the mud, or as someone who can't take a joke. Before long, you'll be joining in with the rest of the crowd and will see the jokes being played on someone else. Because teamwork is so important to firefighters, much of the teasing and the practical jokes are a way to "feel out" new firefighters to see how they'll take it and if they'll be a good sport about it. Of course, if the joking gets out of hand or turns into sexual harassment, you need to seek help from a supervisor.

Learning from Mentors

A mentor is someone you identify as successful and with whom you create an informal teacher-student relationship. Choose your mentor based on what is important to you and on how you define success. Someone can be successful without having achieved certain titles or positions, so keep an open mind when you're looking for a mentor. The purpose of having a mentor is to learn from him or her. Enter into the relationship intending to observe your mentor carefully and ask a lot of questions. The following is a list of things you might be able to learn from a mentor:

- Public interaction skills
- How to study for promotion exams
- What to expect in the firehouse culture
- How to communicate with the chain of command in your department
- In-depth knowledge about equipment and technology used by your department
- Helpful tips for repair and maintenance of equipment and supplies
- What the best firefighter magazines are
- What conferences/classes/training programs you should attend

How to Find a Mentor

You'll probably need to actively search for a mentor in your firehouse, unless someone informally decides to take you under his or her wing and show you the ropes. A mentor can be anyone from a battalion chief to one of your peers. There is no formula for who makes a good mentor; it is not based on title, level of seniority, or years in the department. Instead, the qualities of a good mentor are based on a combination of willingness to be a mentor, level of expertise in a certain area, teaching ability, and attitude.

There are many ways to find a mentor. Here are a couple of techniques you can try for identifying possible mentors in your firehouse:

- Observe people. You can learn a lot about people by watching them. When asked a question, do they take the time to help you find a resolution or do they point you toward someone else who can help you? The one who takes the time to help you resolve your question is the better choice for a mentor. How does the potential mentor resolve problems? In a calm manner? Do problems get resolved? If so, that is probably a good mentor.
- Listen to people who admire your potential mentor. What is it that people admire about him or her? Do the admirable qualities coincide with your values and goals? If you need to learn public presentation skills, you probably shouldn't consider a mentor who is known as a shy and quiet person who becomes tongue-tied when facing a crowd. Instead, look for someone that people describe as personable, calm in public, and who has strong teaching skills.

Don't feel compelled to stick with your mentor forever since career growth may open up new possibilities to you in new areas of specialization. If that happens, you'll probably want to find additional mentors who can show you the ropes in the new environment. However, any former mentors you can keep as friends may not only help you career-wise, but they can also enrich your life in general ways. An experienced firefighter from San Jose, California recollects the following about his first mentor:

> I'll never forget my first mentor in the fire department. I felt so green when I started, and I was afraid of messing up all the time. Then I sought out a senior firefighter who had been with the department for 18 years and began asking him simple questions about how things were run. He was a little gruff at first, but I think he was flattered that I asked him stuff. Pretty soon, he started telling me stories about how things worked around the place, and I got lots of tips and inside information about what the chief was like and how I should respond to the different firefighters and the captain on our shift. I'm still friends with him to this day, even though he retired a long time ago.

Interacting with Supervisors

The number one thing that will help you to interact successfully with a supervisor, whether he or she is a captain or a battalion chief, an incident commander at the site of an emergency, or a fire chief is to follow that person's orders quickly and carefully. Due to the dangerous nature of firefighting, following orders of the superior officers is of utmost importance. Some new firefighters think they can do things better than the way they are currently being done. Be careful about making any brash claims about how great your ideas are when you first begin your firefighting career. The best advice is to look and listen for a good long while to find out the motivations behind the orders and see the results of those orders in action.

When you're not in the midst of an emergency, there is a wide open field of how to best interact with your supervisors. Some fire stations have an informal atmosphere in which everyone jokes with each other and engages in firehouse antics, regardless of rank. Other firehouses are more formal and you need to be on your guard when addressing company officers. You'll get a feel for the atmosphere in your firehouse after a few weeks on the job. Until you know for sure what the atmosphere is, you might want to play it safe and assume it's somewhat formal when addressing your supervisors.

Interacting with the Public

Public interaction is an important part of the firefighter's job. Whether it's an emergency situation or a public fire prevention talk, firefighters are looked on as a highly respected segment of society. Therefore, you don't want to endanger that sense of respect the public has for the office of a firefighter. This is especially important in these days of government downsizing and budget-cutting. Municipal and volunteer fire departments both need to foster public support for their ongoing success. One way for fire departments to do this is through the collective positive actions of firefighters on emergency calls.

Firefighters who offer help and comfort to victims in emergency situations in addition to providing professional emergency assistance generate good will from the citizens being helped as well as from people in the vicinity who witness such help. For example, firefighters who take the time to explain what is happening after a fire occurs or who retrieve someone's prized wedding album from wreckage can go a long way in building respect and support in the community. You'll find that many fire departments focus increasingly on good public relations during an emergency—that builds taxpayer support for municipal departments and healthier donations for volunteer departments. Being a conscientious worker and developing a high level of work performance, along with displaying a caring attitude during emergency situations, will lead you to success.

Qualities That are Rewarded

As you progress through your firefighting career, knowing what qualities are rewarded will give you an edge. There are several things you can do to increase your educational background, technical skills, and effectiveness as a firefighter. Many of the personal qualities that are rewarded in fire departments follow the rules of common sense and include things such as:

- Honesty. Be honest in your dealings with other firefighters, your supervisors, and the public you contact during emergency calls. During emergencies, it's not only your reputation on the line, but that of the entire force.
- Mental Alertness. Being alert when you are on duty can mean the difference between life and death, not only for yourself, but also for the other members of your team and the victims involved.
- Following Orders. As mentioned previously, it's imperative for all firefighters to follow orders in an emergency situation. The incident commander who is giving the orders has more information available to make the calls than anyone else.
- Taking Safety Precautions. Following safety precautions at all times can save lives and reduce injury. Firefighting is a dangerous job, but you can improve the odds by carefully observing all safety rules.
- Learning from Mistakes. Face up to your mistakes and use them to learn the procedures needed for situations that may be similar in the future. Make note of what went wrong during the emergency call and analyze why to ensure it doesn't happen again.
- Good Listening Skills. Firefighters need to listen carefully during the many training and safety sessions that are regularly held in the firehouse as well as to the directions given at an emergency scene so that orders don't have to be repeated or time wasted.

Know When to be Ready

According to the U.S. Fire Administration, fire calls peak at 5:00 to 7:00 p.m. from the surge in cooking-related fires during the dinner period. Broken down by season, residential fires are most frequent during the winter when heating is a dominant cause. For example, the residential fire rate in January is almost twice that of summer months, and the fire death rate in January is triple that of summer months.

Personal Health and Fitness

Firefighters need to maintain good health and physical fitness to perform their tasks well. Some fire departments provide on-site facilities, such as weight training equipment or fitness machines to help firefighters stay in shape. If your department doesn't, consider joining a fitness center nearby or planning regular workouts with other firefighters. You may need to take and pass physical ability tests on a regular basis or to achieve a promotion in some fire departments, so you'll want to be ready. Also, eating balanced meals and getting enough sleep are constant challenges to the modern firefighter. If you are on a work schedule in which you eat meals together at the firehouse, suggest healthful alternatives to the regular diet. Getting in shape and staying fit are important aspects of the firefighter's job, so they should not be ignored.

ADVANCEMENT OPPORTUNITIES

Some firefighters are very satisfied with their job; therefore, they make fighting fires their lifelong career. Others may join up with a municipal fire department as a firefighter and then move into a position of a higher rank, such as lieutenant or captain. The advancement route firefighters can pursue varies depending on the size and location of their fire department, but usually follows this path: level two firefighter, apparatus operator (or engineer), lieutenant or captain, battalion chief, assistant chief, deputy chief, and finally, fire chief. Of course, not everyone advances to become a fire chief, but many firefighters do advance to the level of apparatus operator, lieutenant, or captain.

Advancement opportunities for firefighters often depend on several factors:

- Seniority
- Scores on promotional exams
- Recommendation from supervisor
- Job performance
- Number of openings in higher positions
- Growth of the department
- Education level

You may have all the qualifications, motivation, and skills needed for a promotion in your department, but there may not be any openings at the next level. You can either wait for an opening to occur, or you can apply for a job in another fire department that has more advancement opportunities. According to a firefighter in Florida, it may be worth it to stay in your department and wait for the opening if you really enjoy your work and the people you work with. He says:

> I joined my department at a time when there were already several people who had just been promoted, so I had to wait nine years before I was able to land a promotion to apparatus operator. Then it was another eight years before I made it to lieutenant. Now I see guys getting promoted to those positions within only three or four years of being hired because so many people are retiring or moving on now. It's really a cyclical thing, so if early promotion is extremely important to you, try to find out how many people have been promoted recently in your fire department. If it doesn't look good, you may want to try and transfer to another department right away before you get too settled in. However, if you don't mind the wait, there's great security in staying where you are and not moving around.

You have to determine what is important to you when considering advancement opportunities, so your career choices fit into an overall plan. There are several reasons why you might want to apply to another fire department. Any of the following reasons might apply to you, and by getting another job in a fire department, you can, in essence, give yourself a promotion. Even if it's a lateral move, you can get any one or more of the added benefits from a move:

- Better pay
- Better health benefits and work schedule
- Better training programs
- Better firefighting equipment
- Better camaraderie with coworkers and supervisors
- More room for advancement

Of course, if you land your first job in a great fire department that has lots of benefits and advancement opportunities, then you're all set. You can focus on learning all you can and applying yourself for future promotional opportunities or career challenges in related areas. If you decide to seek advancement in the firefighting field, there are several things you can do to prepare for a promotion.

How to Prepare for a Promotion

Many experienced firefighters study regularly to improve their job performance and to prepare for promotion examinations. In general, firefighters today need more training to operate increasingly sophisticated equipment and to deal safely with the greater hazards associated with fighting fires in larger, more elaborate structures. To progress to higher level positions, firefighters need to acquire expertise in the most advanced firefighting equipment and techniques, building construction, emergency medical procedures, writing, public speaking, management, budgeting procedures, and labor relations.

Fire departments frequently conduct training programs, several colleges and schools offer fire science training programs, and the National Fire Academy sponsors relevant training programs on various topics, including executive development, anti-arson techniques, and public fire safety and education. Some states also provide extensive firefighting training programs at all levels. For instance, in Maryland, the Maryland Fire Service Personnel Qualifications Board offers training and certification for several areas of specialization including but not limited to:

Driver/Operator	Fire Instructor I, II, III, IV
Airport FireFighter	Haz Mat Responder
Fire Officer I, II, III, IV	Haz Mat Technician
Fire Inspector I, II, III	Haz Mat Incident Commander
Fire Investigator	EMS Haz Mat I, II
Public Fire Educator I, II, III	Advanced Exterior Fire Brigade

Taking Promotional Exams

Once you've decided you want to get a particular promotion, you'll need to set up a plan for obtaining that goal. Several things can help your chances of scoring high on a promotion exam. Here are a few of them:

- Get an idea of what will be on the promotional exam. You can ask people who have already taken the exam what areas were emphasized and what books they recommend you study to prepare for the exam. You may be able to get old tests that have been published for students to review relevant material. Or you may be fortunate enough to get a suggested reading list along with the exam materials, although this is rare.

* Set priorities on what material to study. You can't possibly learn every detail about the job you want to obtain, so focus on the most important aspects. If you don't, you can easily get bogged down in wading through details that are not going to be tested on the promotion exam.

* Study test preparation books to find out or brush up on the skills needed to succeed on written exams. For example, look up information on how to handle test anxiety, how to score the highest possible on multiple-choice questions, and how to take tests within specific time limits.

* Make a study schedule several months before the exam and stick to it. Allow sufficient time each day for studying a section of material and don't forget to preview and review the material you study each day. A good study method is to create flash cards and test yourself on key concepts and questions you think may appear on the test.

* Find out if your fire department uses assessment centers to test practical, hands-on aspects of the job you are applying for. If so, talk to people who have gone through the assessment center to get their advice on how you can prepare for this segment of the process. You should also find out if you are allowed to tour the assessment facility to get an idea of what equipment will be used to test you.

Job Descriptions for Advanced Positions

To get a better idea of what could be in store for you in your future firefighting career, take a look at the following job descriptions of key advancement opportunities in the firefighting field.

Apparatus Operator

An apparatus operator is the person who drives the fire truck to emergency calls. They are also referred to as engineers or chauffeurs in some departments. Their skill level goes well beyond merely driving the firetruck, however. They also maintain, inspect, and perform minor repairs on emergency vehicles to ensure a high level of performance. They are responsible for operating pumps, aerial ladders, and/or other equipment during fire suppression calls. Various national certifications for this position are available, including the following:

- Driver/Operator—Pumper
- Driver/Operator—Aerial
- Driver/Operator—Tiller
- Driver/Operator—ARF
- Driver/Operator—Wildland

Apparatus Operators are paid a higher salary than firefighters due to their specialized knowledge and greater amount of responsibility.

Lieutenant or Captain

Lieutenants and captains are referred to as company officers. They supervise firefighters, and they issue orders at the scene of emergencies to their crew. Of course, the size of each lieutenant's or captain's crew varies considerably depending on the size and location of the fire department. However, they all need to be well versed in how to handle emergency situations and how to manage personnel as these two activities make up a large portion of their job. They may also be responsible for training new firefighters in firehouse procedures, inspecting firehouse equipment, and making requests for additional or newer equipment. Lieutenants and captains are normally paid considerably more than firefighters (at least 20-25%) due to their higher level of responsibility and added management duties.

Battalion Chief

Battalion chiefs hold the next higher rank after lieutenants and captains; they are responsible for a group of lieutenants and captains, as well as the firefighters who work under them. Battalion chiefs coordinate and supervise the fire companies under their command during emergency calls and keep communication lines open between lieutenants or captains and superior officers. They are often responsible for recommending personnel for awards; inspecting records, equipment, and personnel in their jurisdiction; issuing purchase orders; and preparing reports of accidents or other noteworthy incidents. They may also assist the fire chief in creating and maintaining departmental budgets and other administrative tasks as needed. Battalion chiefs earn approximately 10-15% more than lieutenants or captains do because of the higher level of responsibility involved in their job.

Deputy Fire Chief or Assistant Fire Chief

Deputy or assistant fire chiefs perform many of the same functions as the fire chief. They are mostly found in large, urban fire departments because fire chiefs need help in departments that employ large numbers of firefighters and cover densely populated areas. Some deputy fire chiefs are responsible for a particular sector of the department, such as operations or training, or they may cover a particular district. See the description under *Fire Chief* below for the types of duties that many deputy and assistant chiefs perform.

Fire Chief

The fire chief is on the top rung of the career ladder that many firefighters are climbing. Fire chiefs are responsible for entire fire departments, including all firefighters, lieutenants, captains, battalion chiefs, and any deputy or assistant fire chiefs. Therefore, their duties are numerous and varied. Specific job duties of fire chiefs vary considerably, depending on the size and type of fire department they are managing. In general, fire chiefs are normally responsible for managing the resources of the department, preparing the departmental budget, commanding multiple-alarm fires, administering laws and regulations in their department, and acting as liaison to public officials for the fire department. Salaries vary greatly for fire chiefs. A fire chief in charge of several thousand firefighters is going to command a much higher salary than one who manages a staff of less than a hundred. Many fire chiefs earn a significant salary due to their many years of experience and high level of education. Indeed, some fire chiefs earn close to or even over $100,000 annually. Of course, fire chiefs in small rural areas earn considerably less.

Sample Job Postings for Advanced Positions

These sample job postings can give you an idea of what type of requirements and salaries are available when seeking advancement opportunities. Of course, salaries vary considerably depending on location and size of fire department, but these descriptions can give you an idea of the possibilities that are out there.

Position:	Firefighter II/Paramedic
Location:	Illinois
Requirements:	Qualified candidates must be between the ages of 21 and 35 and possess EMT-Paramedic certification and three years experience as a full-time firefighter.
Salary:	$34,137-47,912 dependent upon qualifications and experience.

Position:	Deputy Chief of Operations
Location:	Colorado
Requirements:	Bachelor's degree in fire science, fire admin. or related fields, prior supervisory position, 5 years planning or coordinator of a fire & rescue squad.
Salary:	$49,730 annual salary

Position:	Deputy Fire Chief of Testing
Location:	California
Requirements:	Qualified candidates will have worked closely with both career and volunteer personnel; possess fire/emergency command, strategic planning, labor relations, and personnel management skills; residency required w/in 5 mins of district boundaries by date of hire.
Salary:	$54,700 annual salary

Position:	Fire Chief
Location:	Minnesota
Requirements:	Qualified candidates must have an associate degree in Fire Science Technology or a related field. A bachelor's degree is strongly preferred. Must possess strong organizational and communication skills and have experience supervising a fire department that does EMS as well as fire calls.
Salary:	$50,000-61,000 dependent upon qualifications and experience.

CAREER OPTIONS

Fire service is a wide-open and expanding field that offers numerous career choices, whatever your basic interests and abilities may be. In general, firefighter training offers a good, basic background for other fire service careers. Certain career paths involve returning to college or even graduate school for more in-depth study of subjects, such as biology and chemistry, only touched on by firefighting academies. There are also "civilian" career paths in fire service that have specific higher education or certification requirements, but don't necessarily require firefighter training.

Here are descriptions of several fire-related careers that you might be interested in pursuing. Some career options require several years of firefighting experience while others require highly specialized training.

Fire Prevention Specialists

Fire prevention specialists work with a variety of people to teach fire prevention techniques. Many lecture in schools, non-profit groups, civic organizations, and senior living residences. They also work with home and business owners to ensure that vegetation around buildings and homes are cut down and that open spaces between structures are not overgrown with long, dry grass—the fuel of those large wildfires that plague many parts of the country every year.

The priorities for prevention programs are tailored to different locations and purposes. Fire prevention specialists teach people what the leading causes of fires are: cooking, heating, and arson, and what the leading causes of fire deaths are: careless smoking, heating, and arson. These causes are relatively similar around the nation.

Typical Minimum Requirements

The minimum requirements vary from department to department. Some fire departments require that these positions be filled with experienced firefighters through a promotion and application process, which could take several years to complete. Other fire departments are opening up the position of fire prevention specialist to graduates of fire science degree programs who haven't ever served as firefighters. Fire prevention specialists normally have some formal education, public speaking skills, and teaching experience in their background.

Fire Code Enforcement Officers

Fire code enforcement officers oversee the more technical aspects of fire prevention and are similar to fire inspectors. They often review building plans to designate and ensure compliance with fire safety codes and protection systems. They also assess the number and placement of fire exits and establish the maximum number of occupants allowed in a building. Some states refer to their fire inspectors as fire code enforcement officers while others differentiate between the two.

Typical Minimum Requirements

The typical minimum requirements for becoming a fire code enforcement officer vary among departments and states. However, applicants normally need to have either sufficient training from a recognized training program, or several years of experience in the field before attaining the level of fire code enforcement officer.

Fire Marshals

Duties of fire marshals vary greatly depending on what state they work in. The fire marshal position in some states may be appointed by one of the following:

- A state's attorney general
- A state fire board
- A fire prevention commission
- Other governing body

Many fire marshals serve as investigators and investigate fires to determine their origin, whether fire laws have been violated, and whether a fire is the result of criminal negligence or arson. In some states, fire marshals are given powers of subpoena and arrest to investigate the cause of a fire. Marshals may test sites for flammable gases or liquids and are trained to evaluate burn patterns to show where a fire started and how it burned. They report their findings to the district attorney if criminal charges should be filed and are often familiar with laws and court procedures. Many fire marshals also perform inspections of commercial buildings to enforce state fire prevention codes and perform other administrative duties.

Typical Minimum Requirements

The minimum requirements for becoming a fire marshal vary greatly nationwide. But in most states, fire marshals are required to have extensive experience in fire service and public safety or related areas.

Arson Investigators

Arson investigators may work in conjunction with the fire marshal's office or in a fire department's fire prevention division. They investigate the causes of fires and explosions to find out if criminal activity was involved. Their investigative responsibilities are often similar to those performed by fire marshals in some states. Arson investigators use their analytical skills and knowledge of fire science to make judgments and create reports about the fires they investigate. Many arson investigators interview relevant parties to determine the probable cause of a fire. They sometimes testify as expert witnesses in court cases.

Typical Minimum Requirements

Arson investigators are often promoted from a position within a fire department or fire prevention division. Therefore, they often possess firefighting skills or knowledge of fire science practices and procedures. Some states may hire investigators from fire-related fields other than firefighters. Specialized knowledge in how fires are started and how they spread is needed, as well as organization and analytical skills. Most arson investigators have some level of college training.

Hazardous Materials Specialists

Firefighters who deal with dangerous situations involving hazardous materials (called "haz mat" in the field), require specialized training and equipment. Therefore, fire departments usually employ specially trained personnel who are called in to clean up spills or leaks, such as deadly waste dumped from refineries and chemical or nuclear plants.

This growing field is heavily regulated by state and national agencies and requires proper certification, which can be achieved through extension programs at many public colleges. In addition to college training courses, many fire departments take it upon themselves to train their haz mat personnel in their own safety procedures and emergency-response procedures.

Typical Minimum Requirements

Certification in hazardous materials often involves a combination of classroom and hands-on learning from a fire academy, community college, or correspondence course. Some programs offer different levels of certification in haz mat, such as

- Haz Mat Responder—Awareness
- Haz Mat Responder—Operational
- Haz Mat—Technician
- Haz Mat Incident Commander
- Haz Mat Off-Site Specialist, Employees

Crash, Fire, and Rescue Firefighter

Specialized knowledge is needed to become an airport firefighter who deals with airplane crashes and fires. These specialized firefighters conduct rescue efforts of plane crews and passengers in the event of an emergency. They may respond to potential air-crash emergencies by spraying foam on the runway to minimize the chances of an explosion, or to actual air-crash emergencies by spraying chemical solutions or water fog onto the aircraft. They offer emergency medical procedures to victims when needed and may be involved in deactivating aircraft electrical power to prevent explosions. They may be employed by commercial, military, or general airports.

Typical Minimum Requirements

Firefighters who want to specialize in the crash, fire, and rescue area need to obtain training and experience to prepare them for the intricacies of the job. Training programs are offered throughout the nation to help firefighters learn the specialized information needed to respond to air crash, fire, and rescue needs at airports. Firefighters can become certified as an Airport Firefighter by meeting the standards set by the National Board on Fire Service Professional Qualifications, a division of the National Fire Protection Association (NFPA).

Fire Insurance Company Representative

Several opportunities are available for firefighters or others interested in the firefighting field to get hired by fire insurance companies. For example, fire insurance *claim examiners* are needed to analyze fire insurance claims and decide which claims are indeed valid. They also sometimes settle claims after interviewing both claimants and agents. *Claims adjusters* are also needed in the fire insurance area. They are responsible for negotiating settlements after inspecting property damage and other incidents related to a fire. They usually have to prepare comprehensive reports about each case they get. A third representative is called a *fire science specialist*, who may help the insurance company set their rates for fire-related coverage. They also may examine fire prevention methods, such as sprinkler systems, at various places of business and offer suggestions for improving possibly hazardous conditions.

Typical Minimum Requirements

There are no hard and fast rules about who can become a fire insurance company representative. Due to the variety of employers, people with a variety of backgrounds and requirements are needed. In general, you'll need some training or background in fire science and fire investigation work. Some companies may offer you on-the-job-training to fill in the gaps in your background. Many companies look favorably on applicants who have completed an associate degree in fire science or a related area.

Fire Services Instructor

Firefighters who are interested in learning and teaching may wish to become instructors within their fire departments or at a nearby community college or other fire training school. Instructors who work in fire departments are often called *Training Officers.* They provide training to all levels of firefighters, from new recruits to senior firefighters who need training on new materials. Their level of rank depends on the size and location of the fire department, but they are often at the rank of captain or higher. In addition to performing as instructors in a classroom or lab facility, they may also organize training programs for specific groups of people or specific tasks. For example, they may need to organize a training program for the newly hired recruits, or for firefighters who want to apply for the position of apparatus operator or lieutenant. Instructors at colleges or fire academies also perform similar teaching functions and may be involved in organizing or updating training programs.

Typical Minimum Requirements

Since firefighter instructors need a wealth of knowledge in order to teach others, they must have a solid foundation in the subject matter they are teaching. Therefore, they would benefit from several years working as a firefighter before becoming an instructor. For instructors in specialized fields, such as hazardous materials or crash and rescue operations, additional training and field experience are needed. Instructors can obtain certification according to standards set by the National Fire Protection Association (NFPA).

Wildland Smoke Jumper Supervisor

Smoke jumper supervisors coordinate airborne firefighting crews (who are called smoke jumpers) during wildland fires. They examine the location, size, and condition of a wildfire, so they know how many smoke jumpers to employ in each area of the fire. They oversee the process of dropping equipment from aircrafts to the smoke jumpers on the ground as well as retrieving smoke jumpers from the field after a fire is placed under control. Smoke jumper supervisors may get involved in combating actual fires along with their subordinates. They maintain open lines of communication between the smoke jumpers in the field and the crews back at the base of operations. They also train new smoke jumpers in the following:

- parachute jumping
- wildland fire suppression
- aerial observation of fires
- radio communications

Typical Minimum Requirements

Supervisors of smoke jumpers need extensive experience both as smoke jumpers and as wildland firefighters. Since it may take several years to land a job as a smoke jumper due to the extremely intense physical fitness level that is required and the competitive nature of the job, people may need to serve for several years as a seasonal wildland firefighter before becoming a smoke jumper. Then, significant experience is needed as a smoke jumper before applying to become a supervisor.

Forest Fire Warden or Fire Ranger

Fire wardens and rangers are needed in forests and other wildland areas to take fire prevention measures and to scout for dangerous fire conditions. They perform inspections of camp sites, logging areas, and other remote areas to help prevent and report fires. In the case of a forest fire, they may become crew leaders and issue commands on the fireline and in the base camp. They normally examine and maintain firefighting equipment and supplies to ensure accordance with company and government regulations. They may need to give first aid to accident victims.

Typical Minimum Requirements

Typical minimum requirements vary depending on whether you want to work on state, federal, or private lands. Many forest fire wardens and deputies have experience as seasonal wildland firefighters and many become certified through various agencies.

ACHIEVING SUCCESS

After you pass the major hurdle of getting hired by a fire department, you will be well on your way to an exciting and satisfying career. Whether you decide to fight fires or move into a related area within the fire service, you can be proud to be a part of a noble and highly respected profession. If you pursue each step of your career with diligence, dedication, and commitment to excellence, you will be able to achieve great success in your career.

THE INSIDE TRACK

Who:	Jeffrey Cuttitta
What:	Volunteer Firefighter
Where:	Bellmore Fire Department, New York; Oldsmar Fire Department, Florida
How long:	Four years in Bellmore Fire Department; six months in Oldsmar Fire Department

Insider's Advice:

It's very challenging to land a job as a full-time career firefighter because there are so many applicants for every open position and there aren't that many open positions available. My advice is to get as much experience and training as you can. Of course, you should become a volunteer firefighter to learn about the job and get experience before you start applying for career firefighter positions. While you are a volunteer, take advantage of all the free or low-cost training that is available. When I was in Long Island, New York, I went through a fire academy for volunteers that had a lot of great training courses, and they were all free to volunteer firefighters. They offered courses in EMT, ice and cold water rescue, car fires, liquid pit fires, officer's training, pump operation, haz mat courses, and much more. Not all volunteer departments have such a great training program, so if you happen to be in a department that does, be sure to take full advantage of it. Also, get as many certifications as you can while you are a volunteer firefighter. If you have all your certifications, then you can do everything that a paid firefighter can do at fires, including entering burning structures.

Insider's Take on the Future:

I have experience as a volunteer firefighter in two different fire departments, I'm certified as an EMT-Paramedic, and I have Florida state and county firefighter certifications, so I feel confident that I will be able to land a job as a career firefighter in a municipal fire department in the near future. It has been a challenge to go through the rigorous application process, but I have performed well on all the tests and am now waiting to be called from several eligibility lists.

APPENDIX A

In addition to contact information for professional associations, this appendix lists employment recruitment companies and national and regional accrediting agencies. You"ll also find a state-by-state listing of higher education agencies.

PROFESSIONAL ASSOCIATIONS

This appendix contains a list of professional associations and employment recruitment companies that can offer you relevant information related to employment or training as a firefighter, and contact information for accrediting agencies and state higher education agencies.

Professional Associations

Contact any of the following professional associations to find out more information about the firefighting field.

Bureau of Land Management
Department of Agriculture
Washington, DC 20240

International Association of Arson Investigators
300 S. Broadway, Suite 100
St. Louis, MO 63102-2802
314-621-1966

International Association of Black Firefighters
8700 Central Avenue, Suite #306
Landover, MD 20785
202-296-0157

International Association of Fire Chiefs
4025 Fair Ridge Drive
Fairfax, VA 22033-2868
703-273-0911

International Association of Fire Fighters
1750 New York Avenue, NW
Washington, DC 20006

International Association of Fire
Service Instructors
P.O. Box 2320
Stafford, VA 22555
800-435-0005

International Fire Service Training
Association (IFSTA)
Oklahoma State University
Stillwater, OK 74078

National Association of State Fire
Marshals (NASFM)
721 S. Kirkman Road
Orlando, FL 32811
1-800-437-1016

National Association of State Foresters
444 N. Capitol Street, NW
Washington, DC 20001
202-624-5415

National Fire Protection Association
(NFPA)
One Batterymarch Park
Quincy, MA 02269-9101
617-770-3000

National Interagency Fire Center
(NIFC)
3833 South Development Avenue
Boise, Idaho 83705
208-387-5429

Society of Fire Protection Engineers
7315 Wisconsin Avenue, Suite 1225W
Bethesda, MD 20814
301-718-2910; FAX: 301-718-2242

U.S. Department of Agriculture Forest
Service
Fire & Aviation Management
P.O. Box 96090
Washington, DC 20090-6090
703-235-3220

U.S. Fire Administration
16825 S. Seton Avenue
Emittsburg, MD 21727
800-238-3358 / 301-447-1000; FAX:
301-447-1052

U.S. Forest Service
Attn: Firefighting Division
Dept. of Agriculture
Washington, DC 20240

U.S. Park Service
Department of the Interior
Washington, DC 20240

Women in the Fire Service
P.O. Box 5446
Madison, WI 53705
608-233-4768
E-mail: 102754.3630@compuserve.com

Employment Recruitment Companies

These employment recruiting companies offer information (for a fee) to prospective firefighters and to firefighters looking for promotional opportunities. Review each company carefully before you commit to subscribing to a recruitment service. Each company offers slightly different services, and they all charge different rates. Recruitment companies can be especially helpful to prospective firefighters who are looking for openings in other parts of the country from which they reside. Call or write each company for more information.

The Perfect Firefighter Candidate
4475 Dupont Court, Suite #3
Ventura, CA 93003
800-326-8401; FAX: 805-658-7128

Firehire
P.O. Box 1822
Elk Grove, CA 95759
800-755-5891

Public Safety Recruitment
P.O. Box 587
East Jordan, MI 49727
800-880-9018 / 616-536-0155;
FAX: 616-536-2410

IFPRA
708-449-5600, ext. 902
900-225-3400 [Job Hotline costs
$2.95 per minute]

Careers in Fire Service (CFS)
800-997-3373

National Accrediting Agencies

Here is a list of national accrediting agencies for you to contact to find out if your chosen school is accredited. You can request a list of schools that each agency accredits.

Accrediting Commission for Career
Schools and Colleges of Technology
(ACCSCT)
Thomas A. Kube, Executive Director
2101 Wilson Boulevard, Suite 302
Arlington, VA 22201
703-247-4212; FAX: 703-247-4533
E-mail: tkube@accsct.org

Accrediting Council for Independent
Colleges and Schools (ACICS)
Stephen D. Parker, Executive Director
750 First Street, NE Suite 980
Washington, DC 20002-4241
202-336-6780; FAX 202-842-2593
E-mail: acics@digex.net

Distance Education and Training
Council (DETC)
Michael P. Lambert, Executive Secretary
1601 Eighteenth Street, NW
Washington, DC 20009-2529
202-234-5100; FAX: 202-332-1386
E-mail: detc@detc.org

Regional Accrediting Agencies

Not all schools are nationally accredited, but you can find out what schools in your particular region of the country are accredited by a regional accrediting agency. Just contact the accrediting agency that is listed for your region to get a list of schools it accredits.

Middle States

Middle States Association of
Colleges and Schools
Commission on Institutions of
Higher Education
3624 Market Street
Philadelphia, PA 19104-2680
215-662-5606; FAX: 215-662-5950
E-mail: jamorse@msache.org

New England States

Charles M. Cook, Director
New England Association of Schools
and Colleges Commission
on Institutions of Higher Education
(NEASC-CIHE)
209 Burlington Road
Bedford, MA 07130-1433
617-271-0022; FAX: 617-271-0950
E-mail: ccook@neasc.org

Richard E. Mandeville, Director
New England Association of Schools
and Colleges Commission
on Vocational, Technical and Career
Institution (NEASC-CTCI)
209 Burlington Road
Bedford, MA 01730-1433
617-271-0022; FAX: 617-271-0950
E-mail: rmandeville@neasc.org

North Central States

Steve Crow, Executive Director
North Central Association of
Colleges and Schools
Commission on Institutions of
Higher Education (NCA)
30 North LaSalle, Suite 2400
Chicago, IL 60602-2504
312-263-0456; FAX: 312-263-7462
E-mail: crow@ncacihe.org

Northwest States

Sandra Elman, Executive Director
Northwest Association of
Schools and Colleges
Commission on Colleges
11130 NE 33rd Place, Suite 120
Bellevue, WA 98004
206-827-2005; FAX: 206-827-3395
E-mail: selman@u.washington.edu

Southern States

James T. Rogers, Executive Director
Southern Association of Colleges and
Schools
Commission on Colleges (SACS)
1866 Southern Lane
Decatur, GA 30033-4097
404-679-4500/800-248-7701; FAX:
404-679-4558
E-mail: jrogers@sacscoc.org

Western States

David B. Wolf, Executive Director
Western Association of Schools and
Colleges Accrediting Commission for
Community and Junior Colleges
(WASC-Jr.)
3402 Mendocino Ave.
Santa Rosa, CA 95403-2244
707-569-9177; FAX: 707-569-9179
E-mail: ACCJC@aol:com

Ralph A. Wolff, Executive Director
Western Association of Schools and
Colleges Accrediting
Commission for Senior Colleges and
Universities (WASC-Sr.)
c/o Mills College, Box 9990
Oakland, CA 94613-0990
510-632-5000; FAX: 510- 632-8361
E-mail: rwolff@wasc.mills.educ

Obtain Financial Aid from State Higher Education Agencies

You can request information about financial aid from each of the following state higher education agencies and governing boards.

ALABAMA

Alabama Commission on Higher
Education
3465 Norman Bridge Road, Suite 205
Montgomery, Alabama 36105-2310
334-281-1998
-or-
http://www.alsde.edu/
State Department of Education
Gordon Persons Office Building
50 North Ripley Street
Montgomery, Alabama 36130-3901
205-242-8082

ALASKA

http://sygov.swadm.alaska.edu/BOR/
Alaska Commission on Postsecondary
Education
3030 Vintage Boulevard
Juneau, Alaska 99801-7109
907-465-2962
-or-
http://www.educ.state.ak.us
State Department of Education
Goldbelt Place
801 West 10th Street, Suite 200
Juneau, Alaska 99801-1894
907-465-8715

ARIZONA

http://www.abor.asu.edu/
Arizona Commission for
Postsecondary Education
2020 North Central Ave., Suite 275
Phoenix, Arizona 85004-4503
602-229-2531
-or-
http://www.ade.state.az.us/
State Department of Education
1535 West Jefferson
Phoenix, Arizona 85007
602-542-2147

ARKANSAS

Arkansas Department of Higher
Education
114 East Capitol
Little Rock, Arkansas 72201-3818
501-324-9300
-or-
http://arkedu.k12.ar.us//
Arkansas Department of Education
4 State Capitol Mall, Room 304A
Little Rock, Arkansas 72201-1071
501-682-4474

CALIFORNIA

http://www.ucop.edu/ucophome/
system/regents.html
California Student Aid Commission
P.O. Box 510845
Sacramento, California 94245-0845
916-445-0880
-or-
1515 South Street, North Building
Suite 500, P.O. Box 510845
Sacramento, California 94245-0621
916-322-2294
-or-
http://goldmine.cde.ca.gov/
California Department of Education
721 Capitol Mall
Sacramento, California 95814
916-657-2451

COLORADO

http://www.state.co.us/edu_dir/
state_hredu_dept.html
Colorado Commission on Higher
Education
Colorado Heritage Center
1300 Broadway, 2nd Floor
Denver, Colorado 80203
303-866-2723
-or-
http://www.cde.state.co.us/
State Department of Education
201 East Colfax Avenue
Denver, Colorado 80203-1705
303-866-6779

CONNECTICUT

http://www.lib.uconn.edu/ConnState/
HigherEd/dhe.htm
Connecticut Department of Higher
Education
61 Woodland Street
Hartford, Connecticut 06105-2391
203-566-3910
-or-
http://www.aces.k12.ct.us/csde/
Connecticut Department of Education
165 Capitol Avenue
P.O. Box 2219
Hartford, Connecticut 06106-1630

DELAWARE

http://www.state.de.us/high-ed/
commiss/webpage.htm
Delaware Higher Education
Commission
Carvel State Office Building, Fourth
Floor
820 North French Street
Wilmington, Delaware 19801
302-577-3240
-or-
http://www.dpi.state.de.us/dpi/
dpi/dpi.html
State Department of Public Instruction
Townsend Building #279
Federal and Lockerman Streets
P.O. Box 1402
Dover, Delaware 19903-1402
302-739-4583

DISTRICT OF COLUMBIA

Department of Human Services
Office of Postsecondary Education,
Research and Assistance
2100 Martin Luther King, Jr. Avenue, SE
Suite 401
Washington, DC 20020
202-727-3685
-or-
http://www.k12.dc.us/DCPSHP.html
District of Columbia Public Schools
Division of Student Services
4501 Lee Street, N.E.
Washington, DC 20019
202-724-4934

FLORIDA

http://www.nwrdc.fsu.edu/bor/
Florida Department of Education
Office of Student Financial Assistance
1344 Florida Education Center
325 West Gaines Street
Tallahassee, Florida 32399-0400
904-487-0649

GEORGIA

http://www.peachnet.edu/BORWEB/
Georgia Student Finance Authority
State Loans and Grants Division
Suite 245
2082 East Exchange Place
Tucker, Georgia 30084
404-414-3000
-or-

http://www.doe.state.ga.us/
State Department of Education
2054 Twin Towers East
205 Butler Street
Atlanta, Georgia 30334-5040
404-656-5812

HAWAII

http://www.hern.hawaii.edu/hern/
Hawaii State Postsecondary Education
Commission
2444 Dole Street, Room 202
Honolulu, Hawaii 96822-2394
808-956-8213
-or-
http://www.doe.hawaii.edu/
Hawaii Department of Education
2530 10th Avenue, Room A12
Honolulu, Hawaii 96816
808-733-9103

IDAHO

Idaho Board of Education
P.O. Box 83720
Boise, Idaho 83720-0037
208-334-2270
-or-
http://www.sde.state.id.us/
State Department of Education
650 West State Street
Boise, Idaho 83720
208-334-2113

ILLINOIS

Illinois Student Assistance
Commission
1755 Lake Cook Road
Deerfield, Illinois 60015-5209
708-948-8500

INDIANA

http://www.ai.org/ssaci/
State Student Assistance Commission
of Indiana
Suite 500, 150 West Market Street
Indianapolis, Indiana 46204-2811
317-232-2350
-or-
http://ideanet.doe.state.in.us:80/
Indiana Department of Education
Room 229 - State House
Center for Schools Improvement
and Performance
Indianapolis, Indiana 46204-2798
317-232-2305

IOWA

http://www.state.ia.us/government/icsac/
index.htm
Iowa College Student Aid Commission
914 Grand Avenue, Suite 201
Des Moines, Iowa 50309-2824
800-383-4222
-or-
http://www.state.ia.us/educate/
Iowa Department of Education

KANSAS

Kansas Board of Regents
700 S.W. Harrison, Suite 1410
Topeka, Kansas 66603-3760
913-296-3517
-or-
State Department of Education
Kansas State Education Building
120 East Tenth Street
Topeka, Kansas 66612-1103
913-296-4876

KENTUCKY

Kentucky Higher Education
Assistance Authority
Suite 102, 1050 U.S. 127 South
Frankfort, Kentucky 40601-4323
800-928-8926
-or-
http://www.kde.state.ky.us/
State Department of Education
500 Mero Street
1919 Capital Plaza Tower
Frankfort, Kentucky 40601
502-564-3421

LOUISIANA

Louisiana Student Financial
Assistance Commission
Office of Student Financial Assistance
P.O. Box 91202
Baton Rouge, Louisiana 70821-9202
800-259-5626
-or-

http://www.doe.state.la.us/
State Department of Education
P.O. Box 94064
626 North 4th Street, 12th Floor
Baton Rouge, Louisiana 70804-9064
504-342-2098

MAINE

http://www.maine.edu
Finance Authority of Maine
P.O. Box 949
Augusta, Maine 04333-0949
207-287-3263
-or-
http://www.state.me.us/education/
homepage.htm
Maine Department of Education
23 State House Station
Augusta, ME 04333-0023
207-287-5800
TDD/TTY for Hearing-Impaired:
207-287-2550;
FAX: 207-287-5900

MARYLAND

http://www.ubalt.edu/www/mhec/
Maryland Higher Education
Commission
Jeffrey Building, 16 Francis Street
Annapolis, Maryland 21401-1781
410-974-2971
-or-

http://www.maryland.umd.edu/
mde.html
Maryland State Department of
Education
200 West Baltimore Street
Baltimore, Maryland 21201-2595
410-767-0480

MASSACHUSETTS

Massachusetts Board of Higher
Education
330 Stuart Street
Boston, Massachusetts 02116
617-727-9420
-or-
http://www.doe.mass.edu/
State Department of Education
350 Main Street
Malden, Massachusetts 02148-5023
617-388-3300
-or-
http://www.heic.org/
Massachusetts Higher Education
Information Center
666 Boylston St.
Boston, Massachusetts 20116
617-536-0200 x4719

MICHIGAN

Michigan Higher Education Assistance
Authority
Office of Scholarships and Grants
P.O. Box 30462
Lansing, Michigan 48909-7962
517-373-3394
-or-

http://web.mde.state.mi.us
Michigan Department of Education
608 West Allegan Street
Hannah Building
Lansing, Michigan 48909
517-373-3324

MINNESOTA
gopher://gopher.hecb.state.mn.us/
Minnesota Higher Education
Services Office
Suite 400, Capitol Square Bldg.
550 Cedar Street
St. Paul, Minnesota 55101-2292
800-657-3866
-or-
gopher://gopher.educ.state.mn.us/
HOME.HTM
Department of Children, Families,
and Learning
712 Capitol Square Building
550 Cedar Street
St. Paul, Minnesota 55101
612-296-6104

MISSISSIPPI
Mississippi Postsecondary Education
Financial Assistance Board
3825 Ridgewood Road
Jackson, Mississippi 39211-6453
601-982-6663
-or-
http://mdek12.state.ms.us/
State Department of Education
P.O. Box 771
Jackson, Mississippi 39205-0771
601-359-3768

MISSOURI
gopher://dp.mocbhe.gov/
Missouri Coordinating Board for
Higher Education
3515 Amazonas Drive
Jefferson City, Missouri 65109-5717
314-751-2361
-or-
http://services.dese.state.mo.us/
Missouri State Department of
Elementary and Secondary Education
P.O. Box 480
205 Jefferson Street, Sixth Floor
Jefferson City, Missouri 65102-0480
314-751-2931

MONTANA
http://www.montana.edu/~aircj/
manual/bor/
Montana University System
2500 Broadway
Helena, Montana 59620-3103
406-444-6570
-or-
http://161.7.114.15/OPI/opi.html
State Office of Public Instruction
State Capitol, Room 106
Helena, Montana 59620
406-444-4422

NEBRASKA
Coordinating Commission for
Postsecondary Education
P.O. Box 95005
Lincoln, Nebraska 68509-5005
402-471-2847
-or-

http://www.nde.state.ne.us/
Nebraska Department of Education
P.O. Box 94987
301 Centennial Mall South
Lincoln, Nebraska 68509-4987
402-471-2784

NEVADA
http://nsn.scs.unr.edu/nvdoe/
Nevada Department of Education
400 West King Street
Capitol Complex
Carson City, Nevada 89710
702-687-5915

NEW HAMPSHIRE
New Hampshire Postsecondary
Education Commission
2 Industrial Park Drive
Concord, New Hampshire 03301-8512
603-271-2555
-or-
http://www.state.nh.us/doe/
education.html
State Department of Education
State Office Park South
101 Pleasant Street
Concord, New Hampshire 03301
603-271-2632

NEW JERSEY
http://ww.state.nj.us/highereducation/
State of New Jersey
Office of Student Financial Assistance
4 Quakerbridge Plaza, CN 540
Trenton, New Jersey 08625
800-792-8670
-or-

http://www.state.nj.us/education/
State Department of Education
225 West State Street
Trenton, New Jersey 08625-0500
609-984-6409

NEW MEXICO
http://www.nmche.org/index.html
New Mexico Commission on Higher
Education
1068 Cerrillos Road
Santa Fe, New Mexico 87501-4925
505-827-7383
-or-
http://sde.state.nm.us/
State Department of Education
Education Building
300 Don Gaspar
Santa Fe, New Mexico 87501-2786
505-827-6648

NEW YORK
http://hesc.state.ny.us
New York State Higher Education
Services Corporation
One Commerce Plaza
Albany, New York 12255
518-474-5642
-or-
http://www.nysed.gov/
State Education Department
111 Education Building
Washington Avenue
Albany, New York 12234
518-474-5705

NORTH CAROLINA

North Carolina State Education
Assistance Authority
P.O. Box 2688
Chapel Hill, North Carolina
27515-2688
919-821-4771
-or-
http://www.dpi.state.nc.us/
State Department of Public Instruction
Education Building
Division of Teacher Education
116 West Edenton Street
Raleigh, North Carolina 27603-1712
919-733-0701

NORTH DAKOTA

North Dakota University System
North Dakota Student Financial
Assistance Program
600 East Boulevard Avenue
Bismarck, North Dakota 58505-0230
701-224-4114
-or-
http://www.sendit.nodak.edu/dpi/
State Department of Public Instruction
State Capitol Building, 11th Floor
600 East Boulevard Avenue
Bismarck, North Dakota 58505-0164
701-224-2271

OHIO

http://www.bor.ohio.gov
Ohio Student Aid Commission
P.O. Box 182452
309 South Fourth Street
Columbus, Ohio 43218-2452
800-837-6752
-or-
http://www.ode.ohio.gov/
State Department of Education
65 South Front Street, Room 1005
Columbus, Ohio 43266-0308
614-466-2761

OKLAHOMA

http://www.osrhe.edu/
Oklahoma State Regents for Higher
Education
500 Education Building
State Capitol Complex
Oklahoma City, Oklahoma 73105
405-524-9100
-or-
http://www.ogslp.org
Oklahoma Guaranteed Student
Loan Program
P.O. Box 3000
Oklahoma City, OK 73101-3000
405-858-4300 / 800-247-0420
-or-
gopher://gopher.osrhe.edu/
State Department of Education
Oliver Hodge Memorial Education
Building
2500 North Lincoln Boulevard
Oklahoma City, Oklahoma 73105-4599
405-521-4122

OREGON

http://www.teleport.com/~ossc/
home.htm
Oregon State Scholarship Commission
Suite 100, 1500 Valley River Drive
Eugene, Oregon 97401-2130
503-687-7400
-or-
http://www.osshe.edu/
Oregon State System of Higher
Education
700 Pringle Parkway, S.E.
Salem, Oregon 97310-0290
503-378-5585
-or-
http://www.ode.state.or.us/
Oregon Department of Education
255 Capitol Street NE
Salem, OR 97310-0203

PENNSYLVANIA

http://sshe2.sshechan.edu/sshe.html
Pennsylvania Higher Education
Assistance Agency
1200 North Seventh Street
Harrisburg, Pennsylvania 17102-1444
800-692-7435
-or-
P.O. Box 8114
Harrisburg, Pennsylvania 17105-8114
717-720-2075

RHODE ISLAND

http://www.ids.net/ribog/riohe.htm
Rhode Island Office of Higher
Education
301 Promenade Street
Providence, Rhode Island 02908-5720
401-222-6560
FAX: 401-222-6111
E-Mail: RIBOG@uriacc.uri.edu
-or-
Rhode Island Higher Education
Assistance Authority
560 Jefferson Boulevard
Warwick, Rhode Island 02886
800-922-9855
-or-
http://www.ri.net/RIDE
State Department of Education
22 Hayes Street
Providence, Rhode Island 02908
401-222-3126

SOUTH CAROLINA

http://che400.state.sc.us
South Carolina Higher Education
Tuition Grants Commission
1310 Lady Street, Suite 811
P.O. Box 12159
Columbia, South Carolina 29201
803-734-1200
-or-
http://www.state.sc.us/sde/
State Department of Education
803-a Rutledge Building
1429 Senate Street
Columbia, South Carolina 29201
803-734-8364

SOUTH DAKOTA

http://www.state.sd.us/state/
executive/deca/deca.html
Department of Education and
Cultural Affairs
Office of the Secretary
700 Governors Drive
Pierre, South Dakota 57501-2291
605-773-3134
-or-
http://www.ris.sdbor.edu
South Dakota Board of Regents

TENNESSEE

http://www.TBR.state.tn.us
Tennessee Higher Education
Commission
404 James Robertson Parkway
Suite 1900
Nashville, Tennessee 37243-0820
615-741-3605
-or-
http://www.state.tn.us/other/sde/
homepage.htm
State Department of Education
100 Cordell Hull Building
Nashville, Tennessee 37219-5335
615-741-1346 / 800-342-1663 (TN
residents only)

TEXAS

http://www.texas.gov/agency/781.html
Texas Higher Education Coordinating
Board
P.O. Box 12788, Capitol Station
Austin, Texas 78711
800-242-3062

UTAH

http://www.gv.ex.state.ut.us/
highered.htm
Utah State Board of Regents
Utah System of Higher Education
355 West North Temple
#3 Triad Center, Suite 550
Salt Lake City, Utah 84180-1205
801-321-7205
-or-
http://www.usoe.k12.ut.us/
Utah State Office of Education
250 East 500 South
Salt Lake City, Utah 84111
801-538-7779

VERMONT

http://www.vsac.org
Vermont Student Assistance
Corporation
Champlain Mill
P.O. Box 2000
Winooski, Vermont 05404-2601
800-642-3177
-or-
http://www.state.vt.us/educ/
Vermont Department of Education
120 State Street
Montpelier, VT 05620-2501
802-828-3147
FAX: 802-828-3140

VIRGINIA

http://www.schev.edu
State Council of Higher Education
for Virginia
James Monroe Building
101 North Fourteenth Street
Richmond, Virginia 23219
804-786-1690

-or-

http://pen1.pen.k12.va.us:80/
Anthology/VDOE/
State Department of Education
P.O. Box 2120
James Monroe Building
14th and Franklin Streets
Richmond, Virginia 23216-2120
804-225-2072

WASHINGTON

Washington State Higher Education
Coordinating Board
P.O. Box 43430, 917 Lakeridge Way, S.W.
Olympia, Washington 98504-3430
206-753-7850

-or-

http://www.ospi.wednet.edu/
State Department of Public Instruction
Old Capitol Building, P.O. Box FG 11
Olympia, Washington 98504-3211
206-753-2858

WEST VIRGINIA

State Department of Education
1900 Washington Street
Building B, Room 358
Charleston, West Virginia 25305
304-588-2691

-or-

http://www.scusco.wvnet.edu/
State College & University Systems of
West Virginia Central Office
1018 Kanawha Boulevard East,
Suite 700
Charleston, West Virginia 25301-2827
304-558-4016

WISCONSIN

http://www.uwsa.edu/
Higher Educational Aids Board
P.O. Box 7885
Madison, Wisconsin 53707-7885
608-267-2206

-or-

http://www.state.wi.us/agencies/dpi/
State Department of Public Instruction
125 South Wester Street
P.O. Box 7841
Madison, Wisconsin 53707-7814
608-266-2364

WYOMING

http://www.k12.wy.us/wdehome.html
Wyoming State Department of
Education
Hathaway Building
2300 Capitol Avenue, 2nd Floor
Cheyenne, Wyoming 82002-0050
307-777-6265

-or-

Wyoming Community College
Commission
2020 Carey Avenue, 8th Floor
Cheyenne, Wyoming 82002
307-777-7763

PUERTO RICO

Council on Higher Education
Box 23305 - UPR Station
Rio Piedras, Puerto Rico 00931
809-758-3350
-or-
Department of Education
P.O. Box 759
Hato Rey, Puerto Rico 00919
809-753-2200

U.S. DEPARTMENT OF EDUCATION

SSIG Program
Office of Postsecondary Education
Student Financial Assistance Programs
Pell and State Grant Section
U.S. Department of Education
ROB #3, Room 3045
600 Independence Avenue, S.W.
Washington, DC 20202-5447
202-708-4607

Byrd Program
Division of Higher Education
Incentive Programs
Higher Education Programs
Office of Postsecondary Education
U.S. Department of Education
1280 Maryland Avenue, S.W.
Suite C80
Washington, DC 20024

APPENDIX B

ADDITIONAL RESOURCES

Now that you have been through this entire book and know what you need to do to accomplish your goals, look through this appendix for titles that will give you more specific advice on areas with which you need help.

This appendix contains a list of useful books and magazines for your job search.

Books

To find out more about the topics discussed in this book, see the following list of books organized by subject.

Preparing for Firefighter Exams

Firefighter Exam: The South, LearningExpress, 1997 (covers Alabama, Arkansas, Georgia, Louisiana, Mississippi, North Carolina, South Carolina, and Virginia).

Firefighter Exam: New York (State), LearningExpress, 1997.

Firefighter Exam: New York City, LearningExpress, 1997.

Firefighter Exam: Texas, LearningExpress, 1997.

Firefighter Exam: California, LearningExpress, 1997.

Firefighter Exam: New Jersey, LearningExpress, 1997.

Firefighter Exam: Midwest, LearningExpress, 1997 (covers Illinois, Indiana, Michigan, Minnesota, Ohio, and Wisconsin).

Firefighting Training Books

Here are books that contain information about firefighting training.

Clark, William E. *Firefighting Principles and Practices,* 2nd Ed., Penn Well Publishing Company, 1991.

Essentials of Firefighting, 3rd Ed., International Fire Service Training Association (IFSTA), 1992.

Firefighter Entrance Handbook, Davis Publishing Company, 1996.

Firefighting Professional Qualifications, National Fire Protection Association (NFPA), 1992.

Mahoney, Gene. *Fire Department Lieutenant, Captain, Batallion Chief: Score High on Firefighter Promotion Exams,* ARCO Publishing, 1983.

Roberston, James C. *Introduction to Fire Prevention,* 3rd Ed., Macmillan Publishing, 1989.

Steinmuller, Andy. *Unpaid Professional Volunteer Firefighter,* Carlton Press, 1991.

Wieder, Michael. *Fire Service Orientation and Terminology,* 3rd Ed., International Fire Service Training Association (IFSTA), 1993.

Other Firefighting Related Books

You might find one or more of these fire-related books of interest.

Boucher, David. *Ride the Devil Wind: A History of the Los Angeles County Forester and Fire Warden Departments and Fire Protection Districts,* Fire Publications, 1991.

City of Oklahoma City. *Alfred P. Murrah Federal Building Bombing, April 19, 1995, Final Report.* Contains a comprehensive narrative of the events from 9:02 a.m. on April 19, 1995, to the conclusion of the rescue and recovery effort on May 4, 1995, as well as information on follow-up work completed by fire department personnel.

Delsohn, Steve. *The Fire Inside: Firefighters Talk About Their Lives,* HarperCollins, 1996. Contains a collection of interview questions and answers from firefighters across the nation.

Schneider, Edwin F. *A Fire Chief Remembers: Tales of the FDNY,* The Fire Buff House, 1992.

Sineno, John. *The New Firefighter's Cookbook,* Fireside Press, 1996. Contains 200 recipes from New York's Fire Department.

U. S. Fire Administration. *Fire in the United States 1985-1994,* 9th Ed. This 232-page report is a statistical portrait of the fire problem in the United States over the period 1985-1994. It is intended for use by a wide audience, including the fire service, the media, researchers, industry, government agencies, and interested citizens. Includes information on firefighter casualties.

Test Preparation and Study Guides
Read one or more of these books to get additional practice on the basic skills needed to succeed on municipal department or civil service written tests or to help you succeed in a certificate or degree training program.

ACT: Powerful Strategies to Help You Score Higher, 1998 Ed., Simon & Schuster: Kaplan, 1997.

ASVAB: Armed Services Vocational Aptitude Battery: The Complete Test Preparation Guide, LearningExpress, 1997.

Coman, Marcia J. and Kathy L. Heavers. *How to Improve Your Study Skills*, 2nd Ed., NTC Publishing, 1998.

Fry, Ron. *Ron Fry's How to Study Program*, 4th Ed., Career Press, 1996.

How to Study (a part of the *Basics Made Easy* series), LearningExpress, 1997.

Katyman, John and Adam Robinson. *Cracking the SAT and PSAT*, 1998 Ed., Random House: The Princeton Review, 1997.

Practical Math Skill Builder, LearningExpress, 1997.

Reading Comprehension Skill Builder, LearningExpress, 1997.

The Secrets of Taking Any Test (a part of the *Basics Made Easy* series), LearningExpress, 1997.

Vocabulary and Spelling Skill Builder, LearningExpress, 1997.

Distance Education Books
Duffy, James P. *College Online : How to Take College Courses Without Leaving Home*, John Wiley & Sons, May 1997.

Miller, Inabeth, Jeremy Schlosberg, and Adele Scheele. *Kaplan Distance Learning*, Simon & Schuster, November 1997.

Thorson, Marcie Kisner. *Campus-Free College Degrees*, 8th Ed., Thorson Guides, January 1998.

Magazines

Here is a list of fire-related magazines that may be of interest to you.

American Fire Journal
9072 East Artesia Blvd., Suite 7
Bellflower, CA 90706

Fire Chief Magazine
35 Wacker Drive, Suite #700
Chicago, IL 60601-2198

Fire Command Magazine
1 Batterymarch Park
PO Box 9101
Quincy, MA 02269-9101

Fire Engineering Magazine
875 Firehouse Lane, Box 2433
Boulder, CO 80321

FireHouse Magazine
82 Firehouse Lane, Box 2433
Boulder, CO 80321

International Fire Fighter
1750 New York Avenue, N. W.
Washington, DC 20006

Wildfire Magazine
East 8109 Bratt
Fairfield, Washington 99012
509-523-4003; FAX: 509-523-5001

MASTER THE BASICS ... FAST!

WITH THE EXCLUSIVE LEARNINGEXPRESS ADVANTAGE

These books are for you if need to improve your basic skills to move ahead, either at work or in the classroom.
- Become a Better Student — *Quickly*
- Become a More Marketable Employee — *Fast*
- Get a Better Job — *Now*

CLASSROOM TESTED!

Specifically Designed for Classroom Learning OR Independent Home Study!
- 20 easy-to-follow lessons build confidence and skill FAST
- Focus on real-world skills — what you REALLY need to succeed
- Dozens of exercises, hundreds of practical tips, and easy-to-implement steps to SUCCESS

___ READ BETTER, REMEMBER MORE	Item #060-9		___ HOW TO STUDY	Item# 084-6
___ IMPROVE YOUR WRITING FOR WORK	Item #061-7		___ PRACTICAL SPELLING	Item #083-8
___ GRAMMAR ESSENTIALS	Item #062-5		___ PRACTICAL VOCABULARY	Item #082-X
___ THE SECRETS OF TAKING ANY TEST	Item #071-4		___ MATH ESSENTIALS	Item #094-3

SPECIFICATIONS: 7 x 10 • 208 PAGES • $13.95 EACH (PAPERBACK)

ORDER THE BASICS MADE EASY YOU NEED TODAY:

Fill in the quantities beside each book and mail your check or money order*
for the amount indicated (please include $6.95 postage & handling
for the first book and $1.00 for each additional book) to:

LearningExpress, Dept. A040, 20 Academy Street, Norwalk, CT 06850

Or call, TOLL-FREE: **1-888-551-JOBS, Dept. A040** to place a credit card order.

Also available in your local bookstores

Please allow at least 2-4 weeks for delivery. Prices subject to change without notice   *NY, CT, & MD residents add appropriate sales tax

LEARNINGEXPRESS

An Affiliate Company of Random House, Inc.

LEARNINGEXPRESS ®

AT LAST–
TEST PREPARATION THAT *REALLY* WORKS
IMPROVE YOUR SCORES WITH THE EXCLUSIVE LEARNINGEXPRESS ADVANTAGE!

Competition for top jobs is tough. You need all the advantages you can get. That's why LearningExpress has created easy-to-use test prep and career guides, many **customized** specifically for the high-demand jobs in your city and state.

Only LearningExpress gives:

➤ Exclusive practice exams based on official tests given in specific cities and states
➤ Hundreds of sample questions with answers & explanations by experts
➤ Key contacts, salaries & application procedures for individual cities

Plus:

➤ Unique LearningExpress Exam Planners
➤ Critical skill-building exercises in reading comprehension, math, and other commonly tested areas
➤ Detailed career information, including college programs for specific jobs, requirements and qualifications, comprehensive job descriptions, and much more

Thousands of Satisfied Customers Can't be Wrong:

"It's like having the test in advance."
—Ms. J. Kennedy

"Better than the $200 6-week study courses being offered. After studying from dozens of books I would choose yours over any of the other companies."
—Mr. S. Frosh

"Best test-prep book I've used."
—Mr. H. Hernandez

Don't Delay!

To order any of these titles, fill in the quantities beside each book on the order form and mail your check/money order for the full amount* (please include $6.95 postage/handling for the first book and $1.00 for each additional book) to:

LearningExpress
Dept. A040
20 Academy Street
Norwalk, CT 06850

Or Call, TOLL-FREE:
1-888-551-JOBS, Dept. A040
to place a credit card order

LearningExpress books are also available in your local bookstore.

Please allow at least 2-4 weeks for delivery. Prices subject to change without notice   **NY, MD, & CT residents add appropriate sales tax*

June 3, 1998

Order Form

CALIFORNIA EXAMS

___ @ $35.00   CA Police Officer
___ @ $35.00   CA State Police
___ @ $35.00   CA Corrections Officer
___ @ $20.00   CA Law Enforcement Career Guide
___ @ $35.00   CA Firefighter
___ @ $30.00   CA Postal Worker
___ @ $35.00   CA Allied Health

NEW JERSEY EXAMS

___ @ $35.00   NJ Police Officer
___ @ $35.00   NJ State Police
___ @ $35.00   NJ Corrections Officer
___ @ $20.00   NJ Law Enforcement Career Guide
___ @ $35.00   NJ Firefighter
___ @ $30.00   NJ Postal Worker
___ @ $35.00   NJ Allied Health

TEXAS EXAMS

___ @ $35.00   TX Police Officer
___ @ $30.00   TX State Police
___ @ $35.00   TX Corrections Officer
___ @ $20.00   TX Law Enforcement Career Guide
___ @ $35.00   TX Firefighter
___ @ $30.00   TX Postal Worker
___ @ $32.50   TX Allied Health

NEW YORK EXAMS

___ @ $30.00   NYC/Nassau County Police Officer
___ @ $30.00   Suffolk County Police Officer
___ @ $30.00   New York City Firefighter
___ @ $35.00   NY State Police
___ @ $35.00   NY Corrections Officer
___ @ $20.00   NY Law Enforcement Career Guide
___ @ $35.00   NY Firefighter
___ @ $30.00   NY Postal Worker
___ @ $35.00   NY Allied Health
___ @ $30.00   NY Postal Worker

MASSACHUSETTS EXAMS

___ @ $30.00   MA Police Officer
___ @ $30.00   MA State Police Exam
___ @ $30.00   MA Allied Health

FLORIDA EXAMS

___ @ $35.00   FL Police Officer
___ @ $35.00   FL Corrections Officer
___ @ $20.00   FL Law Enforcement Career Guide
___ @ $30.00   FL Postal Worker
___ @ $32.50   FL Allied Health

ILLINOIS EXAMS

___ @ $25.00   Chicago Police Officer
___ @ $25.00   Illinois Allied Health

The MIDWEST EXAMS

(Illinois, Indiana, Michigan, Minnesota, Ohio, and Wisconsin)

___ @ $30.00   Midwest Police Officer Exam
___ @ $30.00   Midwest Firefighter Exam

The SOUTH EXAMS

(Alabama, Arkansas, Georgia, Louisiana, Mississippi, North Carolina, South Carolina, and Virginia)

___ @ $25.00   The South Police Officer Exam
___ @ $25.00   The South Firefighter Exam

NATIONAL EDITIONS

___ @ $14.95   ASVAB (Armed Services Vocational Aptitude Battery)
___ @ $12.95   U.S. Postal Worker Exam
___ @ $15.00   Federal Clerical Worker Exam
___ @ $12.95   Bus Operator Exam
___ @ $12.95   Sanitation Worker Exam
___ @ $20.00   Allied Health Entrance Exams

NATIONAL CERTIFICATION EXAMS

___ @ $20.00   Home Health Aide Certification Exam
___ @ $20.00   Nursing Assistant Certification Exam
___ @ $20.00   EMT-Basic Certification Exam

CAREER STARTERS

___ @ $14.95   Computer Technician
___ @ $14.95   Health Care
___ @ $14.95   Paralegal
___ @ $14.95   Administrative Assistant/Secretary
___ @ $14.00   Civil Service

To Order, Call TOLL-FREE: **1-888-551-JOBS, Dept. A040**

Or, mail this order form with your check or money order* to:
LearningExpress, Dept. A040, 20 Academy Street, Norwalk, CT 06850

Please allow at least 2-4 weeks for delivery. Prices subject to change without notice   **NY, CT, & MD residents add appropriate sales tax*

LEARNINGEXPRESS

An Affiliate Company of Random House, Inc.